Jesus and Elvis

Jesus and Elvis

Creative Resources for Schools and Churches

EDITED BY JOHN McTAVISH

RESOURCE *Publications* · Eugene, Oregon

JESUS AND ELVIS
Creative Resources for Use in Schools and Churches

Resource Publications
An Imprint of Wipf and Stock Publishers
199 W. 8th Ave., Suite 3
Eugene, OR 97401

www.wipfandstock.com

PAPERBACK ISBN: 978-1-5326-6307-9
HARDCOVER ISBN: 978-1-5326-6308-6
EBOOK ISBN: 978-1-5326-6309-3

Manufactured in the U.S.A.   JUNE 18, 2019

To Marion

Who is this that looks out like the dawn,
beautiful as the moon, bright as the sun,
majestic as the starry heavens?

Song of Songs 6:10
New English Bible

Contents

Preface

JESUS AND ELVIS OFFERS a host of creative resources for use in schools and churches. *Jesus* proclaims the book's unabashed gospel-centered content, *Elvis* its unapologetic creative style. The book as a whole should appeal to both the young and the old, wide-eyed seekers, battle-scarred churchgoers, anyone short of the musclebound atheist or bigoted believer. Categories include poems, plays, music, hymns, prayers, a communion service, participatory readings and essays.

"A key," G. K. Chesterton once observed, "has no logic; its only logic is, it turns the lock." That's what these resources do. They invite gospel reflection. They enhance Christian worship. They turn the lock.

Enjoy!

I

Poems

i am a little church
(no great cathedral)

By e. e. cummings

ON THE DAY WORLD War II ended in Europe—*May 8, 1945*—*E. E. Cummings and his wife were driving home from a restaurant in New Hampshire. They happened to notice several people milling about in front of an old green-shuttered, white clapboard Methodist church. Cummings stopped the car, got out and watched for a few minutes. He soon realized that the people were celebrating the end of the war. Mr. Cummings eventually returned to his car, drove home, and in a fit of inspiration composed this poem.*

i am a little church
(no great cathedral)

i am a little church (no great cathedral)
far from the splendour and squalor of hurrying cities
—i do not worry if briefer days grow briefest,
i am not sorry when sun and rain make april

my life is the life of the reaper and sower,
my prayers are prayers of earth's clumsily striving
(finding and losing and laughing and crying) children
whose any sadness or joy is my grief or my gladness

around me surges a miracle of unceasing
birth and glory and death and resurrection:
over my slipping self float flaming symbols
of hope, and I wake to a perfect patience of mountains

i am a little church (far from the frantic
world with its rapture and anguish) at peace with nature
—i do not worry if longer nights grow longest;
i am not sorry when silence becomes singing

winter by spring, I lift my diminutive spire to
merciful Him Whose only now is forever:
standing erect in the deathless truth of His presence
(welcoming humbly His life and proudly His darkness)

As mentioned, E. E. Cummings composed this stirring poem on V. E. Day. The war was over and the poet was naturally relieved that the Axis of Evil had finally been defeated. Even so, Cummings is not celebrating here the defeat of Hitler so much as he is rejoicing in the victory of that love which defeats all sin and suffering and evil and death. This is the cosmic triumph that the church, however small and undistinguished, celebrates:

i am a little church (no great cathedral)
far from the splendour and squalor of hurrying cities

The triumph of God's love brightens the lives of people throughout the world, fundamentally removing all cause for anxiety and sorrow:

—i do not worry if briefer days grow briefest,
i am not sorry when sun and rain make april

The poet goes on to observe that his life is the life of the reaper and the sower. This is not simply an allusion to farming. We all reap and sow insofar as we pursue our daily vocations:

around me surges a miracle of unceasing
birth and glory and death and resurrection:

*Here the poet would seem to be alluding to those human births and glories and deaths and resurrections that are grounded in the birth and glory and death and resurrection of the One who embodies God's love on earth. This is the rock on which all of us, knowingly or unknowingly, stand. The foundation on which—*I wake to a perfect patience of mountains—*the hills and mountains themselves stand fast:*

—i do not worry if longer nights grow longest
i am not sorry when silence becomes singing

The poet concludes with a summons to lift our diminutive spire to merciful Him Whose only now is forever:

. . . erect in the deathless truth of His presence
(welcoming humbly His light and proudly His darkness)

This poem offers an inspiring call to worship, especially if it is followed by a vigorous hymn of praise such as Natalie Sleeth's "Praise the Lord with the Sound of Trumpet," or Rickart's "Now Thank We All Our God." Only be sure to sing with exuberance and joy, even if, no, especially if one is worshipping God in . . .

a little church (no great cathedral)
far from the splendour and squalor of hurrying cities

The Creation

By James Weldon Johnson

JAMES WELDON JOHNSON (1871–1938) retells the Genesis creation saga here with the rollicking cadences and picturesque images of his own Afro-American culture. Google "James Weldon Johnson, The Creation, 2014-04-27" for an excellent rendition of this poem as delivered by the poet himself. Consider working the poem up for a dramatic reading.

The Creation

And God stepped out on space,
And he looked around and said:
I'm lonely—
I'll make me a world.

And far as the eye of God could see
Darkness covered everything,
Blacker than a hundred midnights
Down in a cypress swamp.

Then God smiled,
And the light broke,
And darkness rolled up on one side,
And the light stood shining on the other,
And God said: That's good!

Then God reached out and took the light in his hands,
And God rolled the light around in his hands
Until he made the sun:
And he set that sun a-blazing in the heavens.
And the light that was left from making the sun
God gathered it up in a shining ball
And flung it against the darkness,
Spangling the night with the moon and stars.
Then down between
The darkness and the light
He hurled the world;
And God said: That's good!

Then God himself stepped down—
And the sun was on his right hand,
And the moon was on his left;
The stars were clustered about his head,
And the earth was under his feet.
And God walked, and where he trod
His footsteps hollowed the valleys out
And bulged the mountains up.

Then he stopped and looked and saw
That the earth was hot and barren.
So God stepped over to the edge of the world
And he spat out the seven seas—
He batted his eyes, and the lightnings flashed—
He clapped his hands, and the thunders rolled—
And the waters above the earth came down,
The cooling waters came down.

Then the green grass sprouted,
And the little red flowers blossomed,
The pine tree pointed his finger to the sky,
And the oak spread out his arms,
The lakes cuddled down in the hollows of the ground,
And the rivers ran down to the sea;
And God smiled again,
And the rainbow appeared,
And curled itself around his shoulder.

Then God raised his arm and he waved his hand
Over the sea and over the land,
And he said: Bring forth! Bring forth!
And quicker than God could drop his hand,
Fishes and fowls
And beasts and birds
Swam the rivers and the seas,
Roamed the forests and the woods,
And split the air with their wings,
And God said: That's good!

Then God walked around,
And God looked around,
On all that he had made.
He looked at his sun,
And he looked at his moon,
And he looked at his little stars;
He looked on his world

With all its living things,
And God said: I'm lonely still.

Then God sat down—
On the side of a hill where he could think;
By a deep, wide river he sat down;
With his head in his hands,
God thought and thought,
Till he thought: I'll make me a man!

Up from the bed of the river
God scooped the clay;
And by the bank of the river
He kneeled him down;
And there the great God Almighty
Who lit the sun and fixed it in the sky,
Who flung the stars to the most far corner of the night,
Who rounded the earth in the middle of his hand;
This great God,
Like a mammy bending over her baby,
Kneeled down in the dust
Toiling over a lump of clay
Till he shaped it in his own image;

Then into it he blew the breath of life,
And man became a living soul.
Amen. Amen.

Where Is the Church?

By Ann Weems

St. Paul likened the church to a human body that consists of many limbs and organs. "Now you are Christ's body," the apostle concluded, "and each of you a limb or organ of it" (1 Corinthians 12:12–27). Consider reading this passage and then having individuals stand up wherever they are seated, each person taking turns reciting one of the stanzas of the poem.

Where Is the Church?

The church of Jesus Christ
      is where a child brings a balloon
      is where old women come to dance
      is where young men see visions and old men dream dreams

The church of Jesus Christ
      is where lepers come to be touched
      is where the blind see and the deaf hear
      is where the lame run and the dying live

The church of Jesus Christ
      is where daisies bloom out of barren land
      is where children lead and wise men follow
      is where mountains are moved and walls come tumbling down

The church of Jesus Christ
      is where loaves of bread are stacked in the sanctuary to feed
        the hungry
      is where coats are taken off and put on the backs of the naked
      is where shackles are discarded and kings and shepherds sit
        down to life together

The church of Jesus Christ
      is where barefoot children run giggling in procession
      is where the minister is ministered unto
      is where the anthem is the laughter of the congregation and
        the offering plates are full of people

The church of Jesus Christ
      is where people go when they skin their knees or their hearts
      is where frogs become princes and Cinderella dances beyond
        midnight
      is where judges don't judge and each child is beautiful
        and precious

The church of Jesus Christ
> is where the sea divides for the exiles
> is where the ark floats and the lamb lies down with the lion
> is where people can disagree and hold hands at the same time

The church of Jesus Christ
> is where night is day
> is where trumpets and drums and tambourines declare God's
> > goodness
> is where lost lambs are found

The church of Jesus Christ
> is where people write thank-you notes to God
> is where work is a holiday
> is where seeds are scattered and miracles are grown

The church of Jesus Christ
> is where home is
> is where heaven is
> is where a picnic is communion and people break bread
> > together on their knees

The church of Jesus Christ
> is where we live responsively toward God's coming
Even on Monday morning the world will hear
An abundance of alleluias!

Christmas Trees and
Strawberry Summers

By Ann Weems

WHAT DOES IT MEAN to live one's life as a follower of Jesus and member of his church? Ann Weems offers a poetic, figurative answer to this question. Consider framing your own answer whether in poetry or prose.

Christmas Trees and
Strawberry Summers

What I'd really like is a life of Christmas trees and strawberry
    summers,
A walk through the zoo with a pocketful of bubble gum and a
    string of balloons.
I'd say "yes" to blueberry mornings and carefree days with rain-
    bow endings.
I'd keep the world in springtime and the morning glories
blooming,
But life is more than birthday parties;
Life is more than candied apples.

I'd rather hear the singing than the weeping.
I'd rather see the healing than the violence.
I'd rather feel the pleasure than the pain.
I'd rather know security than fear.
I'd like to keep the cotton candy coming,
But life is more than fingers crossed;
Life is more than wishing.

Christ said, "Follow me."
And, of course, I'd rather not.
I'd rather pretend that doesn't include me.
I'd rather sit by the fire and make my excuses.
I'd rather look the other way,
Not answer the phone,
And be much too busy to read the paper.

But I said YES and
That means risk—
It means here I am, ready or not!

O Christmas trees and strawberry summers,
You're what I like and you are real,
But so are hunger
    and misery
        and hate-filled red faces.

So is confrontation.
So is injustice.
Discipleship means sometimes it's going to rain in my face.

But when you've been blind and now you see . . .
When you've been deaf and now you hear . . .
When you've never understood and now you know . . .
Once you know who God calls you to be,
You're not content with sitting in corners.
There's got to be some alleluia shouting,
>Some speaking out
>Some standing up
>Some caring
>Some sharing
>Some community
>Some risk.

Discipleship means living what you know.
Discipleship means "Thank you, Lord"
For Christmas trees and strawberry summers
And even for rain in my face.

Friday Morning

By Sydney Carter

THE OXFORD DICTIONARY DEFINES *irony as "an expression of meaning, often humorous or sarcastic, by the use of a different or opposite tendency." By this definition, Sydney Carter's poem "Friday Morning" fairly drips with irony. This sometimes causes problems for people who insist on taking everything in their religion literally. (Not that too many literalists are walking around today with an arm cut off or an eye plucked out.)*

The British politician Enoch Powell was sufficiently literalistic that he called for an outright ban on Carter's lyrics in this poem, pouncing especially on the irony-laden line, "It's God they ought to crucify instead of you and me, I said to the carpenter a-hanging on the tree." Of course, in the deepest sense it is God who is a-hanging on the tree alongside the two criminals. This is the point, after all, that the poet is making with all his delicious irony.

Friday Morning

It was on a Friday morning that they took me from the cell
And I saw they had a carpenter to crucify as well.
You can blame it on to Pilate, you can blame it on the Jews,
You can blame it on the Devil, but it's God I accuse.
"It's God they ought to crucify instead of you and me,"
I said to the carpenter a-hanging on the tree.

You can blame it on to Adam, you can blame it on to Eve,
You can blame it on the apple (but that I don't believe).
It was God that made the Devil, and the woman and the man,
And there wouldn't be an apple if it wasn't in the plan.

"It's God they ought to crucify, instead of you and me,"
I said to the carpenter a-hanging on the tree.
Now Barabbas was a killer and they let Barabbas go,
But you are being crucified for nothing here below.
And God is up in heaven, but he doesn't do a thing;
With a million angels watching and they never move a wing.

"To hell with Jehovah!" to the carpenter I said
I wish that a carpenter had made the world instead.
Goodbye, and good luck to you, the road will soon divide:
Remember me in heaven, the man you hung beside.
"It's God they ought to crucify instead of you and me,"
I said to the carpenter a-hanging on the tree.

"Friday Morning" recalls Luke's account of the crucifixion in which two criminals are crucified alongside Jesus (23:26–42). One of the criminals derides Jesus while the other penitently asks to be remembered by him when the Lord comes into his kingdom. The poet then telescopes the words of these two men into the voice of a single person:

"To Hell with Jehovah!" to the carpenter I said
I wish that a carpenter had made the world instead . . ."

Sydney Carter is alluding here to the one line summary of Jesus' life in the Apostles' Creed: "He descended into hell." In agreement with the Creed, Carter is saying that the whole of Jesus' life, and especially his death, can be understood as God descending with us into the hell of human existence, God experiencing in human flesh the utmost of creaturely agony and shame, in order to transform the whole wretched experience into Good Friday.

When the despairing thief cries out: "And God is up in heaven, but he doesn't do a thing," we are reminded of Jesus' cry from the cross: "My God, my God, why have you forsaken me?" (Mark 15:34). Here we have God identifying with us even to the point of experiencing what it means to be forsaken by God.

And when the thief cries out "You can blame it on to Pilate, you can blame it on the Jews, / You can blame it on the Devil, but it's God I accuse," the theodicy question is raised afresh. Why did God create a world in which pain and evil are able to gain such a foothold? We don't know. However, before accusing God of botching the work of creation, we should recall that the Creator at least has chosen from all eternity to go through hell with us so that we should never be there alone, and to go through hell for us so that we should never be there to stay. As the epistle writer puts it: (The crucified) Christ was "destined before the foundation of the world" (1 Peter 1:20).

And so the poem concludes, ironically:

"It's God they ought to crucify instead of you and me,"
I said to the carpenter a-hanging on the tree.

God Is Like My Mommy
(A Special Psalm for Mother's Day)

By Jim Taylor

THE IMAGES OF GOD *in the Bible are almost entirely masculine if only because the writers of the Bible were mainly if not entirely males living in and writing out of a deeply patriarchal age. Their male-centered culture, however, did not prevent Jesus from likening God to a decidedly un-patriarchal Abba or "Daddy" (Mark 14:36), or to an impassioned woman modelled after the mother who turns her house upside down looking for a lost coin (Luke 15:8). This is the tradition that Jim Taylor reflects in retelling the Twenty-third Psalm with feminine imagery.*

Taylor, incidentally, also gives us an engaging chancel drama along feminist lines in the title play of Bedlam in Bethlehem and Other Seasonal Plays *(Samuel French). Bedlam breaks forth in this play when the wise men discover that Mary has given birth to—a girl! A chorus of complaint immediately goes up: "You can't have a female Messiah. No woman will have the strength to drive out evil spirits . . . the power to clear a whole courtyard full of loan sharks and encyclopaedia salesmen . . . a voice that can command obedience even from a thunderstorm." To which Joseph sheepishly replies, "Have you guys, uh, met my wife's mother yet?"*

God Is Like My Mommy
(A Special Psalm for Mother's Day)

God is like my Mommy
My Mommy holds my hand;
I'm not afraid.
She takes me to school in the mornings;
she lets me play in the playgrounds and the parks
she makes me feel good.
She shows me how to cross the streets,
because she loves me.
Even when we walk among the crowds and the cars
I am not afraid.
If I can reach her hand or her coat,
I know she's with me,
And I'm all right.
When I fall down and I'm all covered with mud
and I come home crying,
she picks me up in her arms.
She wipes my hands and dries my tears,
and I have to cry again,
because she loves me so much.
How can anything go wrong
with that kind of mummy near me?
I want to live all my life with mommy,
in my Mommy's home for ever and ever.

A Shining

By Jim Taylor

"It's easy to say what I don't believe in anymore—an all-knowing grandfather God who sits on a cloud somewhere up there, out there, distant but keeping an eye on everything, delivering rewards and punishments, and upsetting things here on earth with what we call 'acts of God.' But then people ask me, 'So what kind of God do you believe in?' And I find prose can't do it; poetry at least comes closer."

—*Jim Taylor*

A Shining

Faces talk around a table
knees warm around a campfire
voices sing in a circle
hands clasp in the darkness
and in between, among, around them
hovers a shining

Eyes cannot see it
ears cannot hear it
fingers cannot touch it
but all feel it
deep, deep within

The shining glows
and pulses
and sings high and clear
and tastes sweeter than honey
whenever two or three
or four or more —
humans or trees
herring or chickadees —
meet and merge
in holy harmony.

Though there is nothing there
everyone knows
something is there
that can't be explained
or explained away

I call it God
What do you call it?

A Valedictory Address to Little People

By Sandra McTavish

"One day, while eating lunch with a group of friends in the cafeteria at work, one woman discussed attending her son's university graduation. She talked about how moving and inspiring the valedictory address was, and how we could all benefit from such inspirational messages. That got me thinking. What valedictory message would I deliver to someone at the beginning of his/her life? What are all my hopes and wishes for a toddler or a newborn? And that's how this poem was born."

—*SANDRA MCTAVISH*

A Valedictory Address to Little People

Dearest wee graduates from
       The womb to the world,
       Or diapers to underwear,
       Or little kid school to big kid school,

My wishes for you
       Are that you live a long, full life —
       Long enough to know the two generations before you and
       Two generations ahead;

That you laugh more than you cry;

And that you always experience freedom;
Never go without the things you really need,
Even if you don't always get the things you want.

I hope you are never afraid in the dark
Or completely alone in the daylight.

May your circle of love extend to a strong circle of people
Who are as caring, compassionate, loyal, and zany towards you
As you are towards them.

I hope you feel comfortable enough in your skin
To dye your hair green (if you want to)
And aren't afraid to wear purple
When everyone else wears grey.

Embrace your body.
Nurture, strengthen, and care for it,
Because you can't trade it in for another.

Share your snacks with the friends who go without
And share your toys—including your favorite ones—
Even with the friends who don't share their favorite toys with you.

Learn all the things you want to know,
And visit all the places you want to see.

Never grow too old
       To jump in puddles,
       To sing in the shower.
       Or (occasionally) to eat ice cream for breakfast.

And before you close your eyes
       For your final sleep on this planet,
       May your last thoughts be,
       "I've lived an incredible life."

Today I Visited Auschwitz

By Sandra McTavish

Hate crimes are on the rise today. What sick passion prompts the human heart to turn with blinding hatred towards Blacks, Jews, Muslims, gays and others? We don't know. We simply know that the hatred is all too often there.

Perhaps this poem can help in a small way by taking us along with the poet on a visit to Auschwitz.

Today I Visited Auschwitz

Today I visited Auschwitz
And realized
That in my 35 years
I have felt no pain
I have shed no tears
I have experienced no sorrow.

I am embarrassed to admit
That I complain
When the hot water in my shower
Turns cold.
And I grumble
When it's raining outside
Causing the May flowers and green grass
To glisten as in a painting
While I am curled under my feathered duvet
In my cozy house.
I even have the nerve to whine
When I have eaten too much
And feel full.

Today I saw a room the size of my cottage
Full of women's hair
That had been cut off after the women had been gassed
And was to be sold and used as stuffing for mattresses.
I saw hundreds of suitcases
With the names of the owners carefully painted
On the sides
The contents emptied and discarded to rich Germans
While the suitcase owners were tortured.
I looked into the eyes of photographed Jews
Who lived a life I can't begin to fathom.

After the three hour tour,
I wanted to vomit;
I wanted to weep.
Instead I prayed to God
Thanking him for my frivolous life.

Ministers Don't Have Sex on Saturdays

By Sandra McTavish

IN POLITE CIRCLES, WE'RE *not supposed to talk about politics, religion, or sex, so readers of this work can only imagine how awkward it is to include this poem by my daughter. She and her mother discouraged me from including it, and I admit it was tempting to hide behind their advice. Nevertheless, the poem is relevant, and current, and did I mention a little awkward for me? She's my 40-something baby girl, and hopefully my wife won't know it's here.*

Ministers Don't Have Sex on Saturdays

On August 19,
> Carrie Baxter is marrying
> Reverend Robert Richardson, the local United Church minister.

And so
> Two weeks before the wedding
The Anglican,
Methodist,
Presbyterian,
And Baptist
Ministers' Wives
Had a tea for the youthful Baxter
In order to explain and introduce her to her future role.

> "Make sure you stand at the back of the church to shake hands
after the service,"
exclaimed the attractive Anglican Mrs. Austen.

> "And always sit in the first or second pew and sing the hymns
boisterously,"
said the musical Methodist's wife.

> "Keep the manse spotless," stated Mrs. Barrington, the benevolent
Baptist.

> "Oh indeed," agreed pragmatic Mrs. Plume, the Presbyterian.
"You never know when your husband will bring parishioners over."

> "And finally . . . oh, I do feel rather embarrassed saying this,"
blushed the Baptist. "But the minster should not have sex on Saturday. It
will distract him on Sunday."

Miss Baxter, the future Mrs. Robert Richardson,
Sipped tea from Mrs. Austen's Royal Albert tea cup and
Smiled thinking to herself:
"Do I dare inform them that
The Reverend Richardson has had sex
The last three Saturday nights and seemed to find it most invigorating."

Who Am I?

By Dietrich Bonhoeffer

IN THE SPRING OF 1939, *Dietrich Bonhoeffer sailed to New York in order to teach at Union Theological Seminary and sit out the coming war. As soon as the young German theologian arrived in the United States, however, he realized that he had made a terrible mistake. If Bonhoeffer was ever going to participate in the rebuilding of his country* after *the war, he surely had to share the coming trials of his people* during *the war. Thus, the theologian took one of the last boats back to Germany, eventually becoming involved in the underground movement that was trying to undermine the Nazi dictatorship from within.*

In 1943, Bonhoeffer was arrested on the grounds of suspicion, and imprisoned. Family connections gave him a good chance of surviving the war. However, these hopes were effectively dashed when his name was linked with the participants of the unsuccessful bomb plot on Hitler's life on July 20, 1944. Sadly, shortly before the war ended, Dietrich Bonhoeffer was taken from his cell and hanged.

Bonhoeffer's poem "Who Am I?" was composed in the spring of 1944 and smuggled out of prison along with other letters and papers that the young theologian had written while awaiting the verdict of his Nazi captors. Discuss the meaning of this poem. Was Bonhoeffer right to leave the United States and return to Germany when he did? What would you have done had you been in his shoes?

And when he got back to Germany, was Bonhoeffer right to join the conspiracy against Hitler and the Nazis? Again, what would you have done, or at least hope you would have done, had you been in his shoes?

Who Am I?

Who am I? They often tell me
I stepped from my cell's confinement
Calmly, cheerfully, firmly,
Like a squire from his country-house.
Who am I? They often tell me
I used to speak to my warders
Freely and friendly and clearly,
As though it were mine to command.
Who am I? They also tell me
I bore the days of misfortune
Equably, smilingly, proudly,
Like one accustomed to win.

Am I then really all that which other men tell of?
Or am I only what I myself know of myself?
Restless and longing and sick, like a bird in a cage,
Struggling for breath, as though hands were
Compressing my throat,
Yearning for colours, for flowers, for the voices of birds,
Thirsting for words of kindness, for neighbourliness,
Tossing in expectation of great events,
Powerlessly trembling for friends at an infinite distance,
Weary and empty at praying, at thinking, at making,
Faint and ready to say farewell to it all?

Who am I? This or the other?
Am I one person today and to-morrow another?
Am I both at once? A hypocrite before others,
And before myself a contemptibly woebegone weakling?
Or is something within me still like a beaten army,
Fleeing in disorder from victory already achieved
Who am I? They mock me, these lonely questions of mine.
Whoever I am, thou knowest, O God, I am thine!

Mary's Christmas

By Charlotte Martinson Gronseth

THE POET IMAGINES MARY *gazing at her newborn child and reflecting on the meaning of his birth. Discuss the gospel insights that Mary expresses in this poem.*

Mary's Christmas

The birthing is over.
And the pain.
The babe securely swathed
lies sleeping.
And Joseph.
Now the sinking back
onto fresh straw,
and the pondering.

What has happened here
tonight?
This tiny hand, fingers curling
tightly round my thumb,
was this the hand that placed
the stars in heaven
And set each one
aflame?

This mouth that puckers,
smiles
at the warm moist breath
of the curious ass,
did it in the beginning
breathe life into clay?

Infant of my body,
angels praised you.
And the shepherds,
strangely shy and reverent,
hoarsely whispering their
excitement
so as not to frighten,
lingered and adored.
So must I.

Strange . . . I cannot deny
an apprehension
tugs.
Yet I am too weary
for such riddles now.
It is late.
The rooster soon will crow.
I, too, must sleep.

Yes, Virginia, There Is a God*

By Belden C. Lane

WE MAY TIRE OF all those well-meaning but all too predictable diatribes against the commercialization of Christmas. Yet something surely needs to be said about the Christmas overkill. And this poem says it well.

Yes, Virginia, There Is a God*

AND there were in the same country
Shepherds abiding in the field
Not a creature was stirring
Not even a
Mouse

And this shall be a sign unto you
Let's put Christ back into Christmas
Wrapped in swaddling clothes
Dreaming of a white Christmas
Away in a manger

Happy holidays and for a wonderful new year
A multitude of the heavenly host
Praising God and saying
Only 13 shopping days
Until xmas

So you better watch out, you better not pout
While shepherds watched their flock by night
The special Christmas sale at Macy's
Will go into its third
Week

The little lord jesus lays down his sweet
Seasons greetings and silver bells
God of God, Light of Light, true God
Avoid the christmas
Rush

Begotten not made, of one substance with
Optimist christmas trees
Glory to God and on earth
A partridge in a pear tree
Born of the virgin mary
They shall call his name
Here comes Santa Claus
Which being interpreted is
Five gold rings
Four calling birds

Conceived of the Holy Ghost
Two for a dollar seventy nine
In excelsis deo
Like a bowful of
Jelly

*HE'S JUST VERY HARD TO RECOGNIZE

The Women

Anonymous

IN TELLING US THAT Jesus *"grew in wisdom"* (Luke 2:52), the gospel writer implies that Jesus needed to grow. And surely that need was apparent on the day the Canaanite woman begged him to heal her psychiatrically ill daughter (Matt. 15:21f, Mark 7:24f). Jesus resisted the plea on the grounds that he had been sent *"only to the lost sheep of Israel."* The woman nevertheless persisted while Jesus, for his part, remained adamant: *"Let the children be fed first; it is not fair to take the children's bread and throw it to the dogs."*

The woman now took these shockingly prejudicial words and turned them to her own advantage: *"Sir, even the dogs under the table eat the children's scraps."* Finally the penny dropped. Jesus saw her point and grew in wisdom. The Lord grew! The next thing we know the little Canaanite girl had been healed.

Why do we mention this? Simply because *"The Women"* is a contemporary reminder that women loom large in scripture. Only their voices aren't always heard by those of us who may still have some growing to do.

The Women

A wandering tribeswoman was my mother.
In Egypt, she bore slaves.
Then she called to the God of our mothers:
Sarah, Hagar, Rebecca, Rachel, Leah.
Praise God Who Hears, Forever.

A warrior, judge, and harlot was my mother.
God called her from time to time
To save and liberate God's people:
Miriam. Jael, Deborah, Judith, Tamar.
Praise God Who Saves, Forever.

A Galilean Jew was my mother.
She bore a wonderful child
To be persecuted, hated, and executed.
Mary, mother of sorrows, mother of us all.
Praise God Who Gives Strength, Forever.

A witness to Christ's resurrection was my mother.
The apostle to the apostles.
Rejected, forgotten, proclaimed a whore.
Mary of Magdala, vanguard of women-church
Praise God Who Lives, Forever.

An apostle, prophet, founder, and teacher was my mother
Called to the discipleship of equals,
Empowered by the Sophia-God of Jesus.
Martha, Phoebe, Junia, Priscilla, Myrta, Nympha, Thecla.
Praise God Who Calls, Forever.

A faithful Christian woman was my mother.
A mystic, witch, martyr, heretic, saint, uppity woman.
A native American, a black slave, a poor immigrant,
An old hag, a wise woman.
May we, with her, in every generation
Praise God Who Images Us All.

Looking to the Light

By Patricia Wells

THE POET HERE SUGGESTS *that even beyond the grave we are still somehow recognizably ourselves and not simply phantom spirits. This hope is based on "the shimmering miracle," the "divine sleight of hand" manifested in the resurrection of the rabbi and friend of the women, the one who sends them "dancing down the road, laughing, arms raised, fingers snapping, feet light in the cool morning dust . . ."*

Looking to the Light

Death will be no more; mourning and crying and pain will be no more, for the first things have passed away." Revelation 21:4

In the dim beginning
of human time
a woman leans over a grave,
carefully placing a spear
and bowl of wild grain
by her husband's side,
knowing the bones, bowl, spear
will remain in the dirt
but signalling a hope
that his spirit will rise
into an embodied paradise.

In a clear blue dawn
the women are dancing
down the road,
laughing, arms raised,
fingers snapping,
feet light in the
cool morning dust,
gleeful that their rabbi
and friend
has escaped the cruelty of Romans,
Sadducees, and Death,
by a shimmering miracle,
a divine sleight of hand,
freed into a future
of God's choosing,
hopeful that where
he has gone
they may one day follow.

Jesus and Elvis

By John Updike

JESUS AND ELVIS! THE *two well-known "kings" have made a strong impression over the years, the one as a Gentile hip-swinging performer, the other as a Jewish freelance preacher. Both in their day were profoundly controversial, and paid for it with early deaths. Elvis was done in by "pills and chiliburgers." Jesus was tortured to death by his religious and political opponents. Even so, the two kings continue to rule the world in significant ways: Elvis through his music, Jesus as the embodiment of God's love.*

The enigmatic conclusion of the poem recalls the words of Jesus: "Because I live, you all will live" (John 14:19). In other words, because the crucified and risen Christ lives, we all live even though we die. And because we all live, our culture, including the music of Elvis, lives. In other words: "He [Jesus] lives. We live. He [Elvis] lives."

Conclude the session by singing or playing some of Elvis's greatest hits: "Always on My Mind," (note the Royal Philharmonic Orchestra's presentation on YouTube of this song with Elvis), "Love Me Tender," "Can't Help Falling in Love," and—why not?—"You Ain't Nothing but a Hound Dog."

Also sing some of the hymns glorifying the crucified and risen Christ, hymns such as "Fairest Lord Jesus," "Lift High the Cross," "What Child Is This," and again, why not, "Jesus Loves Me."

A special word to schools: Don't underestimate the hymns.

A special word to churches: Don't underestimate Elvis.

Jesus and Elvis

Twenty years after the death, St. Paul
was sending the first of his epistles,
and bits of myth or faithful memory—
multitudes fed on scraps, the dead small girl
told *"Talitha, cumi"*—were self-assembling
as proto-Gospels. Twenty years since pills
and chiliburgers did another in,
they gather at Graceland, the simple believers,

the turnpike pilgrims from the sere Midwest,
mother and daughter bleached to look alike,
Marys and Lazaruses, you and me,
brains riddled with song, with hand-tinted visions
of a lovely young man reckless and cool
as a lily. He lives. We live. He lives.

Perfection Wasted

By John Updike

This sonnet was composed by John Updike in the wake of his mother's death. Ah, John Updike's mother. I used to visit Linda Updike on her farm in Pennsylvania when I was taking summer courses at Princeton Theological Seminary in nearby New Jersey. Over the years a lovely, warm friendship developed, helped no doubt by the fact that I very much appreciated her son's work.

"Perfection Wasted" is a beautiful sonnet in which that grieving son sings the praises of his beloved mother.

A helpful poem for use at funerals.

Perfection Wasted

And another regrettable thing about death
is the ceasing of your own brand of magic,
which took a whole life to develop and market—
the quips, the witticisms, the slant
adjusted to a few, those loved ones nearest
the lip of the stage, their soft faces blanched
in the footlight glow. Their laughter close to tears,
their tears confused with their diamond earrings,
their warm pooled breath in and out with your heartbeat,
their response and your performance twined.
The jokes over the phone. The memories packed
in the rapid-access file. The whole act.
Who will do it again? That's it: no one,
imitators and descendants aren't the same.

Seven Stanzas at Easter

By John Updike

"THE EASTER MESSAGE," KARL Barth claimed, "tells us that our enemies, sin, the curse and death, are beaten. Ultimately they can no longer start mischief. They still behave as though the game was not decided, the battle not fought; we must still reckon with them, but fundamentally we must cease to fear them any more." What Barth said in prose, Updike says here in poetry. The resurrection is the miracle in which all our old enemies, sin, the curse and death are ultimately beaten. Without the resurrection the human family is lost; with the resurrection we are snatched from death and given the assurance of God's eternal love.

But, mark well, bodily resurrection! We are not Platonists. It is not as though the body dies while the soul lives on. The whole person dies. If there is a resurrection, however, the whole person, body and soul, awakens to new life in the mysterious dimension of eternity.

The "if" in the first stanza of this poem—if he rose at all—recalls St. Paul's pivotal preposition: "If Christ has not been raised, then our proclamation has been in vain . . . If Christ has not been raised, your faith is futile and you are still in your sins . . . If for this life only we have hoped in Christ, we are of all people most to be pitied" (1 Corinthians 15: 14-19).

On an aesthetic note, notice how beautifully patterned the poem is. How the first and fourth lines of each stanza rhyme, and how the extra long expository line is followed by a short, hushed, climactic fourth.

This poem sings!

Seven Stanzas at Easter

Make no mistake: if He rose at all
it was as His body;
if the cells' dissolution did not reverse, the molecules reknit,
        the amino acids rekindle,
the Church will fall.

It was not as the flowers,
each soft spring recurrent;
it was not as His Spirit in the mouths and fuddled eyes of the
        eleven apostles;
it was as His flesh: ours.

The same hinged thumbs and toes,
the same valved heart
that—pierced—died, withered, paused, and then regathered
        out of enduring Might
new strength to enclose.

Let us not mock God with metaphor,
analogy, sidestepping, transcendence,
making of the event a parable, a sign painted in the faded
        credulity of earlier ages:
let us walk through the door.

The stone is rolled back, not papier-mâché,
not a stone in a story,
but the vast rock of materiality that in the slow grinding of
        time will eclipse for each of us
the wide light of day.

And if we will have an angel at the tomb,
make it a real angel,
weighty with Max Planck's quanta, vivid with hair, opaque in
        the dawn light, robed in real linen
spun on a definite loom.

Let us not seek to make it less monstrous
for our own convenience, our own sense of beauty,
lest, awakened in one unthinkable hour, we are embarrassed
        by the miracle,
and crushed by remonstrance.

Saved By Grace

By Karl Barth

THERE ARE TWO WAYS *of preaching the gospel: the legalistic way (if you believe, you will be saved) and the evangelical or gospel way of preaching the gospel (you have already been saved: therefore believe).*

In this excerpt from a sermon by Karl Barth delivered to inmates in a Swiss prison, the famous theologian can be found presenting the gospel in a clear, evangelical, gospel-like way.

Barth is widely regarded as one of the most if not the *most important theologian of modern times. Yet many preachers, both conservative and liberal, still tend to preach the gospel in a more legalistic than gospel-like way.*

Why?

Barth's text is Ephesians 2:5: "By grace you have been saved."

We have arranged the concluding words of the sermon in the poetic form of verse.

Saved by Grace

Dear brothers and sisters, where do we stand now?

One thing is certain:
the bright day *has dawned*,
the sun of God *does shine*
into our dark lives,
even though
we may close our eyes to its radiance.

His voice *does call* us from heaven,
even though
we may obstruct our ears.

The bread of life *is offered* to us,
even though
we are inclined to clench our fists
instead of opening our hands
to take the bread and eat it.

The door of our prison *is open,*
even though,
strangely enough,
we prefer to remain
within.

God has put the house in order
even though
we like to mess it up all over again.

By grace you have been saved!—

this is true, even though we may not believe it,
may not accept it as valid for ourselves
and unfortunately in so doing
may forego its
benefits.

Why should we want to forego the benefits?
Why should we not want to believe?
Why do we not go out through the open door?
Why do we not open our clenched fists?
Why do we obstruct our ears?
Why are we blindfolded?

Honestly, *why?*

One remark in reply must suffice.

All this is so because perhaps
we failed to pray fervently enough
for a change within ourselves,
on our part.

That God is God,
not only almighty but merciful and good,
that he wills and does what is best for us,
that
Jesus Christ died for us to set us free
that
by grace,
in him,
we have been saved—

all this need *not* be a concern of our prayers.

All these things are true apart from
our own deeds and prayers.

But to believe, to accept,
to let it be true for us,
to begin to live with this truth,
to believe it not only with our minds
and with our lips,

but also with our hearts

and with all our life,
so that
our fellowmen may sense it,

and finally
to let our total existence
be immersed in this great divine truth,
by grace you have been saved,
this is to be the concern of our prayers.

No human being has ever prayed for this in vain.

If anyone asks for this,
the answer is already being given
and faith begins.

And because no one has asked for this in vain,
no one may omit praying like a little child
for the assurance that God's truth,
this terrible, this glorious truth,
is shining even today,
a small, yet increasingly bright light.

By grace you have been saved.

Ask that you may believe this
and it will be given you;

seek this, and you will find it;

knock on this door,
and it will be opened to you.

This, my dear friends, is what I have been privileged and empowered to
tell you of the good news as the word of God today.

Amen.

2

Plays

Four Chancel Dramas

THE FOUR CHANCEL DRAMAS *in this chapter are all available for production purposes through Samuel French's New York or London offices.*

"Take Me" by Jim Taylor finds a contemporary Mary re-living her life with her son moments before his death. I have seen actresses in their fifties, but also in their teens, move audiences to tears portraying Mary in this play.

Patricia Wells' "The Face of Jesus" gives us two modern-day prisoners on death row who remind us of Jesus and Barabbas. This play lends itself to dramatic readings as well as theatrical performances.

"The Scarecrow" is a powerful Christian allegory written by the Canadian playwright Allan Stratton when he was sixteen years old. The two false messiahs in this play represent everyone from Hitler to the local church bigot. Their zealous followers finally turn on each other in a way that not only hastens their deaths but causes the Christ figure in the play, the Scarecrow, to die afresh.

"The Mouse's Discovery" is an easy-to-produce Christmas pageant for children of all ages. This play features some very human-looking mice who happen to be on the spot one night as shepherds gather, a king plots, and a special child is born.

(1) Take Me

By Jim Taylor

Mary *enters, running, looking over her shoulder to see if someone or some-thing else is coming.*

Mary: I know they'll be coming this way. Soon they'll—oh, I wish I could be any place but here. Why do I punish myself by . . . We mothers ought to be put out of our misery! There's just no justice being a mother. I mean, we spend our lives for our children, and look what happens. They hurt you. They reject you. They leave you to pick up the pieces after they've gone off to do their own thing—whatever that is.

And then, when they get into trouble, you find you hurt just as much as if they were still your little baby.

When I look back on all that's happened, when I think how excited I was before he was born, when I think of all the plans and expectations I had for him—and now . . .

You know, that old man was right. He warned me that it would be like a sword piercing my heart. I never really knew what he meant until now. *(Pause)*

Oh, I guess there were bad times before this—of course there were! Frankly, if any of us knew what it would be like, we'd have never applied for the job. Seriously. You couldn't pay anyone enough to be a mother! How much would you have to be paid, to be on duty 24 hours a day, every day of the year? To get up in the middle of the night when they're babies, to wait up half the night for them when they're teenagers, and then even when they've grown up and left, you still lie awake at night worrying about the scrapes they've gotten into?

Who would take on that kind of job? For any amount of money? *(Slight pause)*

Of course, at the time you don't realize what's ahead. *(Pause; Mary be-comes momentarily girlish)*

You know, on the whole, I think the nine months of pregnancy may have been the best part of being a mother. Aside from what the smell of coffee did to me! Really, I sometimes think we women were meant to be pregnant. I felt so good while I was carrying him. I even wrote poetry—me! Poetry! Listen.

"My soul doth magnify the Lord.
And my spirit hath rejoiced in God my Saviour.
For he hath regarded the low estate of his handmaiden:
For behold, from henceforth all generations shall call me blessed.
For he that is mighty hath done to me great things;
And holy is his name." *(Pause)*

So what if he kicked me once in a while—there was that wonderful feeling—of something new, something utterly unique growing inside me . . . a kind of awe that this should be happening to me . . .

The first time he moved, inside me, I'll never forget it. Never. And everybody said I was just blooming with health! But it doesn't last. It can't last. The child has to be born. I felt as if I was being torn apart, hour after hour, gasping, screaming, my flesh tearing . . .

Later my breasts filled until they ached . . . Not that nursing wasn't a pleasure! It was wonderful, that part. It was so satisfying, for both of us. I remember thinking, this must be what motherhood is all about. Then he gets teeth! From then on, it's all downhill.

After a while, kids just don't want you to care about them any more. Every day is just another fight.
    "Where are you going?"
    "Out."
    "Who with?"
    "My friends."
    "Oh. That's good . . . I thought you might be going out with your enemies."
    "Aw, Mum, get off my back, will ya!"
    "Well, what are you going to do?"

"What difference does it make? Don't you trust me any more?"
"Of course I trust you, dear. I just don't trust those friends!"

So after a while you let him grow up his own way. He's got to learn from his own mistakes, right?

Then you start hearing the stories. The time he went downtown. The weekend at the lake. You know he's getting into trouble, even if it isn't really his fault. It's the people he hangs around with. Bums—that's all they are. Just low-brow, riff-raff, working class bums!!

I don't know—it's almost as if kids had to deliberately reject everything you ever taught them, everything you stand for. As if they had to hurt you, wound you, cut you to the heart. (*Pause*)

I tried to talk with him. I tried to reason with him. But talking turns into arguing, and arguing turns into fighting. Oh, what's the use? (*Marches off and then suddenly wheels around, voice breaking with incredulity*) And then, one day, that's it—he's gone. Your baby. Your little boy. On his own. And you stand there, like the only tombstone on a hill, and you hear the wind whistling around you and . . . I don't know, you feel so empty . . . so alone.

After my son left . . . I found out where he'd gone, what he was up to. I tried to convince him to give up this, this obsession of his. Come home, I told him. I still have your old room. It's still yours, any time you need it. I can take care of you. I can! (*Pause*) He turned and walked away.

I don't know where it all went wrong. (*We hear the rattling of chains, the shuffling of feet*) Oh my God! They're coming. They're going through with it. They're actually going to . . . I don't know why they wouldn't just let him go. He's a good boy. A good boy! Sure, he broke a few rules. He did a few foolish things. Who doesn't? But he was never mean. He was never cruel. He never set out to hurt anyone—except me—no, no, not even me! He just had to do what was right, even if everyone else thought it was wrong.

And for that—that's all—they're going to crucify him, right here on this garbage dump; crucify him like a common criminal, like someone who had killed, or raped, or robbed! My . . . my son . . . my little boy . . . my darling . . . So many people cared about him—(*We hear the rattling of chains again and the thud of a cross being planted in the ground*)

It's him. It *is* him. I was hoping it would be a mistake . . . You can't do this. It isn't fair. Don't you see? He couldn't have stopped doing what he believed in any more than I could have stopped being his mother. He couldn't have lived with himself if he had compromised his principles. Is that wrong? Is it wrong to care about others? And he did care. He really did. And it made a difference. They needed him. They needed him a lot more than those rich successful beasts! Those exploiters! They just wanted to use him for their own purposes. They wanted him to be a puppet on their string. They're the ones who are doing this to him, because . . . because he made them ashamed of themselves. Oh no . . . ! No, no! Not nails. Not, not nails. No, no, no . . . ! (*Sound of nails being hammered is heard; hammering continues as Mary buries her head in her hands and sinks to the floor*).

Those lovely hands. He'll never use them again. To shape wood. To hold a child. To touch his mother's cheek. (*Mary moves to the back of the chancel, her arms outstretched as if she herself was being crucified*) He didn't do anything wrong! (*Hammering starts up again*) Stop it! Stop it. Stop it!!!!! (*Hammering continues as Mary's body registers the blows. Pause*)

He doesn't deserve this. He's a good boy . . . He's my . . . my . . . Oh, God. (*Mary comes down stage and kneels, speaking straight out to the audience*) Why did he have to pay the price? He didn't do anything wrong. *I* was wrong. I was selfish and thoughtless. (*Turning to address Jesus on the cross*)

Oh, my son, my son, how could I have disbelieved you? I should have believed you. I do believe you. Now . . . now I do. (*Arms outstretched to God above*) Oh God, why didn't you take me instead? Take me now O Lord. Take me . . .

(*Slow fade and blackout*)

(2) The Face of Jesus

By Patricia Wells

Cast

Jesus

Barabbas

Barabbas: Welcome to death row.

Jesus: Death row?

Barabbas: Yeah, there's just four of us here. You don't play poker, do you? We could get up a game.

Jesus: Who are the other two?

Barabbas: Couple buddies of mine. Got caught stealing. Just thieves. Whadja in for?

Jesus: I'm not sure.

Barabbas: You mean you're innocent? Welcome to the club.

Jesus: I think it's called Aggravated Conspiracy to Cause Dissension.

Barabbas: Hey, that's a new one. Who dreamed that up?

Jesus: Our religious leaders.

Barabbas: No kiddin'! Oh well, Guess what I'm in for?

Jesus: Murder?

Barabbas: Hah.

Jesus: Sedition?

Barabbas: What does that mean?

Jesus: It means you tried to overthrow the government. You killed people, you raped. You . . .

Barabbas: Okay, okay, whatever. Anyway, my name's Jesus. What's yours?

Jesus: That's my name, too.

Barabbas: My old man was Abbas. So I'm really Jesus bar Abbas. You can call me Barabbas. Everybody else does.

Jesus: I'm just Jesus. Jesus bar Joseph.

Barabbas: Your old man was Joseph?

Jesus: In a way.

Barabbas: Whaddya mean in a way? Was he or wasn't he?

Jesus: It's kind of complicated.

Barabbas: Yeah, sure. *(pause)* Hey! Why do you keep looking at me like that?

Jesus: Like what?

Barabbas: You despise me, don't you?

Jesus: Not at all.

Barabbas: You've got that holier-than-thou look in your eyes. I can tell. Just because I'm a murderer and you didn't kill nobody. You think you're better than me, don't you?

Jesus: Not at all.

Barabbas: Okay . . . You feel sorry for me then.

Jesus: Well, yes I do.

Barabbas: Well, I don't need your pity! Don't waste your precious pity on me, Jesus bar Joseph. Who are you to pity anybody anyhow? We're both gonna hang, you know! And when they take us down we'll both be dead as doornails.

Jesus: That's why I feel sorry for you.

Barabbas: Yeah, well, like I say, I don't need your pity. You can feel sorry for yourself.

Jesus: It's not exactly pity.

Barabbas: What is it then?

Jesus: Try compassion.

Barabbas: Compassion? What's that?

Jesus: Well, love. You know what love is, don't you?

Barabbas: Yeah, well my definition of love probably ain't the same as yours buddy.

Jesus: Did you love your mother?

Barabbas: 'Course I did. *(pause)* But I wasn't the only one.

Jesus: Tell me about her.

Barabbas: My old lady?

Jesus: Yes.

Barabbas: Put it this way. I don't know who my father was except he was some guy called Abbas. I only had one father . . . But I sure had lots of uncles. If you get my drift.

Jesus: I get your drift.

Barabbas: What about *your* old lady?

Jesus: My mother?

Barabbas: Yeah. What's she like?

Jesus: She's a sweet brave lady who long ago wrapped me in swaddling clothes and laid me in a manger. She's the woman who sits behind a computer all day making data entries. She's the woman who works in a home for people with AIDS and holds their hands when they die. She's the woman in India who sweeps the streets all day with a broom . . .

Barabbas: (*interrupting*) Hah. What about the lady who sits on a bar stool with a drink in her hand and says, "Hi ya handsome? New in town?" Is she your mother?

Jesus: Yes.

Barabbas: Then maybe we're brothers.

Jesus: Maybe we are.

Barabbas: You really are 'round the bend up the whatjimacallit, aren't you? But, hey. You just may be crazy enough to get us out of here. Let's escape!

Jesus: There is no escape.

Barabbas: 'Course there is! It's the oldest trick in the book, and we've got a guard dumb enough to fall for it. Look. You pretend to be sick. Just start gagging or croaking or something and I'll call the guard. He comes running, sees you lying on the floor, bends over, I grab him, take the keys, kill him and we're outta here.

Jesus: I told you, Barabbas. There is no escape. For either of us.

Barabbas: Oh, come on. We're gonna die anyway. What's to lose? We can at least—What's the matter with you!!! Standing there like a helpless idiot. A crazy, stupid, helpless (*pause*) Hey! . . . Where'd you say you was from?

Jesus: Nazareth.

Barabbas: Nazareth . . . a hillbilly from . . . Hey, wait a minute. You're Jesus, right? Jesus of Nazareth . . . Oh my God . . . You're the guy everybody's talking about. The nutcase that's been going 'round the countryside stirring up all kinds of trouble . . . Hey guys! My cellmate's a preacher! Whadja think of that? (*to Jesus*) Just don't preach at me, huh?

Jesus: I don't preach at anyone.

Barabbas: Whadja mean? Whaddaya do then?

Jesus: I tell the truth.

Barabbas: Oh yeah. Love your neighbor. Love your enemy. I've heard it all.

Jesus: There's one thing more.

Barabbas: What's that?

Jesus: Love your God.

Barabbas: God! What's he ever done for me?

Jesus: He just gave you a friend.

Barabbas: Who? (*Jesus smiles.*) You? (*Jesus smiles again.*) You're no friend. You're no . . . help at all.

Jesus: Wait and see.

Barabbas: The only thing we've got waiting for us is our last meal. Hey, didja put in your order yet? Whadja gonna get?

Jesus: I'm not hungry.

Barabbas: Don't be nuts. We can get anything we want. Grab it while you can.

Jesus: I had my last meal last night.

Barabbas: You did? Whadja have?

Jesus: Bread and wine.

Barabbas: That all?

Jesus: Those who had it with me will remember.

Barabbas: Yeah? And who was that?

Jesus: A dozen of my closest friends.

Barabbas: Some friends. Where are they now?

Jesus: They're waiting.

Barabbas: Waiting? For what?

Jesus: To see what will happen to me.

Barabbas: I can tell you what's gonna happen. You're gonna *die*. Same as me. Sunset tomorrow. Poof. We'll be gone. (*scornfully*) "Waiting to see what will happen . . ." You're not even brave, are you? There're tears in your eyes. I can see 'em from here. All that preacher talk 'bout God and heaven and the silly old angels . . . You're just as scared as the rest of us.

Jesus: It's true, Barabbas. My eyes *are* filling up. I can tell you I'm not looking forward to what they're going to do to us tomorrow. But I also feel terrible for my people, for Jerusalem, for the whole . . .

Barabbas (*overlapping*): There you go again. Getting all soppy and delusional. I tol'ja. I don't need your pity. What I need is co-operation. Come on! Shake a leg. Let's trick that dumb guard and get outta here. Whaddya say?

Jesus: I think you know what I'm going to say.

Barabbas (*losing it*): Why are you so stubborn? (*to the guards*) Oops. Sorry. Sorry, governor. I'll keep my voice down. (*to Jesus*) Don't shout, they say, everybody needs their sleep. Great. Few hours from now we're all gonna be six feet under sleeping forever. (*losing it again*) In the meantime, why don't you shut your own . . . Oops. Sorry. Sorry again . . . What? No, no, I wasn't . . . What . . . Whaaat??

(*long pause*)

Okay, let me get this straight. You're saying one of us can walk outta here, free as a bird, no strings attached, just . . . *Go* . . . Ha. Ha . . . I can tell you who that's gonna be. Goody two shoes over there. The little preacher boy who never hurt a flea. *Why are you tormenting me like* . . . ? Whaaat? Whadja say? . . . It's not him? . . . It's me . . . I can go free? . . . The cell door's wide open. I just walk out and . . . ? No, look. There's gotta be a mistake. I mean . . . let's face it I'm as guilty as hell 'n everybody knows it. My friend over there, he might be a little funny in the head but he never hurt nobody. We all know that.

Jesus: Whatever happened to the hardened criminal, Barabbas?

Barabbas: (*ignoring Jesus, his attention fixed on the jailer*): What's that? No more gabbing. Just . . . get the hell out of here?

Jesus: There's no escape, Barabbas. But I'm glad you're free.

Barabbas (*laughing*): You're darn right I'm free. I'm outta here, buddy. I'm *history!*

(*Barabbas exits*)

Jesus: Father . . . I pray for his soul. He needs you. In his crazy, mixed-up, violent way he's crying out for you. Touch his heart and give him peace. (*pause, then calling to the guard*)

All right! . . . I'm ready.

(*Jesus exits down a long aisle. A long pause, then . . .*)

Barabbas (*laughing*): Well, I'm back! Everybody else is gone and I'm still kicking. Howdja like that!

(*There's a mood change now as Barabbas becomes serious for once.*)

Okay, okay. I know it's not all fun and games. I stayed around, you know, and watched my cellmate go down. It wasn't a pretty sight. Some of his friends were there. Also some women. I think one of them might have been his mother. They were talking, but I couldn't hear what they were saying. And then, I don't know . . . I just had this crazy urge to . . . to go up to the cross and touch his poor, bleeding, godforsaken body . . . Just for a second.

He looked at me and . . . I think he tried to say something but all he could do was kinda nod his head. Then somebody shouted my name and I got outta there fast . . .

I don't know what to make of it all . . . And now there are these crazy rumours that he could be alive again. I honestly can't believe it. And yet a really weird thing happened to me just the other night.

I was prowling the streets and I came across a body lying in a gutter. Turned out it was our old guard of all people. He'd been attacked, I guess, and I decided to have the honor of finishing him off.

But just as I raised my dagger, he opened his eyes and groaned and honest to God . . . I found myself looking into the face of Jesus.

I know. Crazy. But there it was.

I turned and ran. I'm still kind of running, still trying to figure it all out.

(*pause*)

How 'bout you? You anywhere closer to the truth? I hope so . . . I'd hate to think my buddy died in vain.

(3) The Scarecrow

By Allan Stratton

Cast

The Scarecrow

The Young Man

Hen

Cow

Bunny

Cat

Horse

The Elegant Gentleman

Piggy

Dog

Fox

Lamb

Goose

Time

Now

Setting

A Field

When lights go up, the stage is bare but for two things. One is a piece of pipe two to three feet long and one inch wide which is placed widthwise on the stage, dividing it into two segments. At rear center stage is the scarecrow hung up on a cross. Bright, circus-like music up. Enter Young Man. *Music down.* Young Man *is a combination of insolence, sarcasm and callousness. He observes the stage, scarecrow. As he does this, enter* Hen, Cow, Bunny, Cat,

Horse. *They stand erect and are dressed in white turtlenecks, black trousers. When music goes down they freeze in a line or tableau, staying always on stage right.*

Young Man: Ahhhhh. Ah, yes. Yes indeed. Indeed yes. This will do perfectly. There's grass and a briar patch for Bunny (*Pointing to Scarecrow*), some sort of a native God to back up my orders and (*Pointing to pipe*) a pipe with which to build a system of drainage. (*To audience*) After all, I am an enlightened despot. In case you might be interested, it was about twenty-five years ago that I was hatched by parents not noted for their ingenuity. Which accounts for why they simply called me Young Man. Now in addition to me they used to have some useless farmland. I say "used to" because they decided to die two years ago on the grounds of better late than never. I was despondent. I mean after funeral expenses I was completely broke. And it was at that point in my life that I decided to become a Messiah or some such thing. Anything to keep off welfare. So here I am along with my loyal disciples: Cat, Cow, Bunny, Horse, and my favorite disciple, Hen. Hen has been very loyal. She has delivered one hard-boiled egg every day—which we share.

Hen (*Proudly*): Cluck, cluck, cluck.

Young Man: She is the bravest, brightest and best of us. And as such, is being made into a pie next Sunday. (*Music up, down*)

Hen: Corn, seed, wire meshing.

Cow: Hay, grasses, cedar hedges.

Cat: Milk, cream, catnip nibbles.

Horse: Plough, furrows, autumn threshing.

Bunny: Corn, carrots, briar patches.

All: In the farm sleep, eat and pray,

And worship Young Man every day.

And if we do as he commands

Fetch, carry, obey, worship

He will take us to a land of

Bunny: Carrot trees

Cat: Lakes of milk.

Hen: Banks of grain

Horse: Roads of corn

Cow (*Solemnly*): And lots and lots of crab apples. (*Music up and down. Pastoral march. Enter in a line Piggy, Dog, Fox, Lamb, and Goose*)

Piggy: Swill, mud hole, potato peelings.

Dog: Pointing, hunting, fetching, retrieving.

Fox: Chicken hatches, coat of sheen.

Lamb: Wool, darning, winter stockings.

Goose: Grain, downing, nursery rhymes. (*Abruptly enter Elegant Gentleman, carrying suitcase*) [*Note: The two groups do not yet notice each other. The second group is dressed in black turtlenecks and white slacks and trousers*]

Elegant: Hup two. Attention. None of you lost? No one's died on me? Excellent. Good show! Nobly done. This looks to be the place. There's grass and a mud hole over there for Piggy. And my, my, what have we here? Why, I do believe it's a native God of some sort. And here's a piece of pipe with which to bash the heads of passing strangers. Now listen all. You see this quaint figure that someone's hung out to dry? Very well. This is the Great God Funny Fingers, noted for his hands of straw. Now, you will remember that last week you worshipped the Great God Anthill. Now this week you will worship the Great God Funny Fingers. And of course like Anthill, Funny Fingers agrees with everything I say.

Scarecrow: Peace on earth, good will toward all.

Elegant (*Slowly, cold, measured*): Quiet, now. (*To audience*) My name is Elegant Gentleman and I am the 43rd in a long list of heirs to the family fortune. A dotty family. My mother was one of those who believed that with faith you could fly, and so, plucking up her faith in both hands she stood atop a flagpole, jumped—and flew. Straight down. Therefore since I could no longer believe or pray in all truthfulness, I decided to become a Messiah, which had the added advantage of not having to go to church.—And it was something to do until the other 42 heirs died off. My father lasted a bit longer—until he was ready for his pension. But then, just when he would have been useful, he remembered to die too and there was I, an unemployed Messiah. I have since gathered these five disciples: Piggy, Dog, Fox, Lamb and Goose. Goose is my favorite since she is too stupid to question me. (*Music up, down. Animals of both Messiah's mingle as a matter of habit*)

Goose: All right now girls. Get your bridge partners. Quack. Order now, girls. Don't forget to take out the jokers. Haha. Ha. Has anyone seen the Jack of Spades? Oh good. Quack quack quack. We're going to have such a fun time. Isn't that nice. Ha ha ha. Of course. Yes. Oh, dear me! I feel so excited. (*Hen, Goose, Lamb and Cat* form *partners*) Why, this is such a fun group!

Cow (*Mournfully*): Who do I play with?

Goose (*Deep concern*): Oh my dear yes. (*Brightly*) How about you play solitaire this time round.

Fox: All those for poker. (*Bunny, Horse, Piggy, Dog, Fox, in a group, play with imaginary cards*)

Dog (*To Horse and Bunny*): I suppose you two have heard all about the Great God Funny Fingers.

Bunny: The Great God what?

Dog (*Solemnly*): Shhh. Not so loud. The Great God Funny Fingers. Ruler of the barnyard and everything else.

Horse: No!

Dog: Yes. He knows what everyone does and thinks. And if we don't do what Mr. Elegant Gentleman wants the Great God Funny Fingers will tell on us and we will be punished.

Bunny: How?

Dog: Shhh.

Bunny (*Whispering*): How?

Dog: With a giant whip. The skies will open, a giant whip will descend and our skins will be flayed from our backs to make lampshades for the Great God Funny Fingers.

Horse: No!

Dog: Yes.

Bunny: Where is he?

Dog (*Whispering*): Over there.

Scarecrow: Peace on earth, good will toward all. *(The five sit petrified and then begin to cautiously play. When this is over, Music up, down. Young Man and Elegant Gentleman begin surveying the land. They don't notice each other for a time until they are level with each other)*

Young Man: Who are you?

Elegant: My name, sir, is Elegant Gentleman the 43rd. And what might yours be?

Young Man: Mr. Young Man.

Elegant: I see, I see. How fascinating. I like that name. It's got that homespun sound.

Young Man: Thank you.

Elegant: Of grandeur it smacks not, but it does have a homespun sound. Do you have any brothers or sisters?

Young Man: None. Do you?

Elegant: Yes. Forty-two. Are you just passing through?

Young Man: No. I live here with my animals. I own this whole area.

Elegant: Why, what a coincidence! So do I.

Young Man: You must be mistaken, sir.

Elegant: Not in the least. I am the one and only Messiah. And what might you be? A lawyer, a teacher, a shepherd to tell me what I own? I, sir, am a Messiah.

Young Man: Wow! *(Sarcastic)* For how long?

Elegant: For one year, two weeks, five hours.

Young Man: Well, sir. I have been a Messiah for one year, two weeks, and *six* hours. I'm afraid you'll just have to move.

Elegant: Perhaps, but I'm going to remain located right here, on this side of the pipe.

Young Man: Very well, but see you stay there. Otherwise I shall be forced to call on the Great God Potato Sack to damn you.

Elegant: Nonsense. And who is this Great God Potato Sack?

Young Man *(Pointing to Scarecrow)*: There.

Elegant: The Great God Potato Sack??? Well, of course I wouldn't want to disillusion you, seeing as how you are a Messiah and all, but I feel it my duty to inform you that that is not the Great God Potato Sack at all. That, sir, is the Great God Funny Fingers.

Young Man: Why, not at all! I distinctly heard him say "I am the Great God Potato Sack."

Elegant: That's what you may think you heard, but Funny Fingers and I are old friends. Why, whenever I'm in trouble, I just call him up and say, "Hello, F.F., is that you?", whereupon he replies, "Why, my dear E.G., how are you these days?"

Young Man: I'm afraid you've been getting a wrong number. Why, ever since I was a child . . .

Scarecrow: Peace on earth, good will toward all.

Young Man: One more word and you'll be a mattress. (*Music up—the two face each other in hate, then turn and retire to their various sides. The card games break up and the two sides move apart*)

Bunny (*In fear, to Young Man*): Is it true that this is the Great God Funny Fingers?

Young Man: No. That is the Great God Potato Sack who damns those who call him otherwise. And if you ever call him the Great God Funny Fingers, the clouds will open and a giant scissors of fire will descend and snip off your tail. But to those who do as I say, he is King.

Cow: Will he give lots and lots of crab apples?

Young Man: Yes, and much more. So remember that and pray often, or he will come in a mountain of fury most terrible to behold.

Scarecrow: Peace on earth good will toward all.

Young Man (*Cold, measured*): Silence. (*On the other side of the stage Piggy, Dog, Fox, Lamb and Goose are kneeling to Scarecrow. Music up, down, quickly*)

Animals of Elegent Gentleman:
To the Great God Funny Fingers
Oh, little man with mildewed mind

And heart of molding straw;
With button eyes and nettled nose
Whose mouth a sewn smile,
How can you now love a world
That's desolate and cold?

Scarecrow:
I love with eyes that cannot see.
With nose that cannot smell.
With mouth that cannot change,
With hearing children
In the glen.

Animals of Young Man:
Oh little man with
Mildewed mind
And heart of molding straw,
How do you abide the crow
That rapes the furrows that you tend
And tears your flesh for nests
Of weeds and nettles, mud and straw.

Scarecrow:
I abide with eyes that would but weep
With nose that would but bleed
With mouth that would but cry
With hearing children
In the glen.

(Music up, down. The worshippers remain down in a freeze. Elegant Gentle-
man prepares to hit an imaginary ball with an imaginary golf club. He hits
it into the audience, scans the sky for it, then with no luck snaps his fingers

and puts down another imaginary ball from his pocket. Young Man begins to whistle)

Elegant: I don't like whistling . . . It irritates me . . . Will you stop it?

Young Man: Pardon? Is that you, Elegant Gentleman?

Elegant: Yes it is.

Young Man: Good morning. *(Goes back whistling)*

Elegant: Will you stop that! You are giving me indigestion.

Young Man: But such a charming ditty.

Elegant: Funny Fingers has expressly forbad whistling. Why, just the other day he called me up on the phone and said, "Hello E.G. Would you mind reminding everyone that I expressly forbid whistling. Tell them: Thou shalt not whistle. It gives me indigestion." So you see, Funny Fingers has forbidden whistling.

Young Man: Potato Sack hasn't.

Elegant: You will one day see the error of your ways. Funny Fingers will damn you. *(He prepares to hit the other golf ball)*

Young Man *(Sarcastically):* Wow! Just what does the Great God Funny Fingers allow?

Elegant: Oh, a great number of things. *(Swinging the club)* Elegance for one. *(Following the ball with his eyes)* Whenever we have tea together Funny fingers always says, "I say, E.G., you are looking elegant today. Glad to see it." He also allows golf, for example. F.F. is mad about golf.

Young Man: Well, considering as how you are a Messiah, you don't seem to be doing excessively well.

Elegant: Not doing well? Tut, tut. On the contrary. While on the surface it might appear that I am getting nowhere, I am actually doing exceptionally well. You see, Funny Fingers doesn't allow holes-in-one or birdies either for that matter. "Thou shalt not get holes-in-one or birdies either for that matter" to use his exact words. Funny Fingers never gets holes-in-one, and by the happiest of coincidences, neither do I. Do you play golf?

Young Man: No. The Great God Potato Sack doesn't allow it. Besides, I'm allergic to golf balls. Whenever a golf ball comes near me I break out in a rash.

Elegant *(Putting an imaginary ball on the ground)*: Tut, tut. How distressing. But you don't mind if I play do you?

Young Man: Not at all. But I do feel compelled to warn you that I must report you to Potato Sack. He's allergic to golf balls too.

Elegant *(Putting his ball on the ground onto Young Man's side of the pipe)*: Tut. Tut. How distressing.

Young Man: You have just tapped your ball onto my side of the pipe.

Elegant *(Overly polite)*: Dear me! But that can be fixed, can't it? *(Moves pipe further stage right)*

Young Man: I should hate to be the one to bring to your attention a glaring oversight on your part.

Elegant: Good.

Young Man: However, truth will out! You have just moved the pipe over a rather large expanse of territory.

Elegant: Shame on me. But I'm certain it was there a minute ago.

Young Man *(Putting it farther back Stage Left than its original position)*: Well, you're wrong.

Elegant *(Putting it back Stage Right)*: Well, I'm right. *(They move pipe back and forth in a tug of war until Scarecrow speaks, then pipe is dropped and their anger is turned on Scarecrow)*

Scarecrow: Peace on earth, good will toward all.

Elegant: Desist.

Young Man: Dry up. *(Musical chord)*

Animals of Young Man: Potato Sack a nettled king

Sing praises to His Name.

Funny Fingers—Anti-sack

False, fleeting shadow god.

Those of Elegant: Great Funny Fingers arms out-stretched

To hug a morning sky

Potato Sack—Antifingers

On a charcoal crucifix.

Hen: A pigsty harridan is Fingers.

Piggy: No, a friend to lonely pigs.

Dog: An ox-eyed knave Potato Sack.

Cow: But no, a gentle friend for us.

Cat: A silly goose is Funny Fingers.

Goose: He's a friend to creatures true.

Fox: A steel trap is Potato Sack.

Bunny: No, he's gentle, kind and true.

Horse: A scurvy weakling filled with fleas. Is this fly named Fingers? Odd.

Lamb: No. He's loving, gentle, true.

Scarecrow: Peace on earth, good will towards all.

Those of Elegant: Down with Potato Sack. Down with Potato Sack.

Those of Young Man: Down with Funny Fingers. Down with Funny Fingers. (Music up, down. The two leaders come to the center. They nod very formally. Young Man picks up pipe, begins to move off)

Elegant: And where might you be going with that pipe, boy?

Young Man: Were you speaking to me? My name goes without saying to my friends, but to you it is Mr. Young Man.

Elegant: What a homespun name. (Sneering) Where are you going with that pipe?

Young Man: I am planning on building a drainage system for the animals. Potato Sack and I.

Elegant: Well, seeing as it's my pipe . . .

Young Man: But it's my pipe. Ask Potato Sack.

Elegant: I happen to have bought it from Funny Fingers. It's a matter of record.

Young Man: Let me see the receipt.

Elegant: I ate it.

Young Man: Then I'm using this pipe.

Elegant: I suppose you realize that my land extends as far left *(he points Stage Right)* as you take that pipe.

Young Man: Which is precisely why I am building this little underground edifice across there. *(Points across Elegant's land)*

Elegant: I'm afraid you're wrong. If you don't give it back to me, I won't ever let you dig the ditch.

Young Man: In which case Piggy will be refused use of my mud hole.

Elegant: In which case Bunny will not be able to use my briar bush.

Scarecrow: Peace on earth, good will towards all.

Young Man: Try it. Then we'll see who's boss.

Elegant: You just dig a trench on this side of the pipe and I will.

Young Man: *(Putting his toe across the line and kicking a furrow)* Through that shall the first trickle of water flow.

Elegant: Bunny is henceforth forbidden in my briar bush.

Young Man: I warned you. I warned you. Bunny, Hen, Cat, Horse and Cow—the Great, High and Mighty God Potato Sack himself has come to me in a vision of thunder and fire. He tells us to destroy the Fingerites who are deceitful, dangerous and cowardly.

Scarecrow: Peace on earth.

Elegant: Fox, Piggy, Lamb, Goose and Dog—the Great High and Mighty God Funny Fingers himself has come to me in a vision of thunder and fire. He tells us to destroy the Potatoites who are deceitful, dangerous and cowardly.

Scarecrow: Good will towards all.

Young Man: I propose a game of Kick the Baby in the Gut.

Elegant: Agreed. *(To audience)* I was once a college champion. *(Animals line up in two opposing lines like chess pieces. The positions to which they move are chosen arbitrarily on the imaginary chess board which serves as a* *metaphor for the battleground. The leaders turn away from the battle and stand like bookends to it. Ominous music throughout.)* Your move.

Young Man: Bunny to briar patch four. *(Bunny moves to an imaginary 'chess square')*

Elegant: Fox to briar patch four. *(Fox mimes killing Bunny by strangling him; Bunny falls)*

Young Man: Hen to mud puddle three.

Elegant: Fox across to mud puddle three. *(Fox attacks Hen; Hen falls.)*

Young Man: Horse's hoof to Fox's head. *(Fox down)* Cat to tree six.

Elegant: Goose to pond one. Lamb to field two.

Young Man: Cat to pond one. *(Both go down)*

Elegant: But you forgot she couldn't swim. Pig to mud seven.

Young Man: Horse to field two. *(Lamb down)* Cow to hay five.

Elegant: Dog chase cow into pond one. *(Cow down)*

Young Man: Horse's hoof to Pig's snout. *(Pig down)*

Elegant: Dog chase horse into tree. *(Both down. Scarecrow dies; his head lolls forward)* And now Dog move in for checkmate. *(Pause)* I said Dog move in for checkmate. (**Young Man:** *turns around)*

Young Man: My Horse crushed your Dog as he rammed into the tree.

Elegant: Our animals?

Young Man: They're all dead.

Elegant: Funny Fingers? Potato Sack?

Young Man: They're both dead.

Elegant: Anything?

Young Man: Dead. *(Slow fade to black)*

(4) The Mouse's Discovery

A Christmas Pageant for Children of All Ages

By Marion McTavish

Cast

(Reading parts):
Head Palace Mouse
Head Magi Mouse
Head Field Mouse
Head Stable Mouse

(Miming parts):
King Herod
*Magi**
*Palace Mice**
*Shepherds**
*Field Mice**
*Angels**
Joseph
Mary
Baby

*can be any number or sex

Set

A lectern stands on one side of the stage where the Head Mouse sits, and a pulpit on the other side where the Head Field Mouse sits. In front and to the side of the pulpit is a Christmas tree. Behind the lectern is a throne on which King Herod sits. Across the back is the choir loft or elevated chairs on which the Angels sit.

The first verse of familiar Christmas songs are sung throughout the presentation. The audience remains seated, and joins in the singing. Suggested songs include: "Deck the Halls," "We Three Kings," "It Came Upon a Midnight Clear," "While Shepherds Watched Their Flocks by Night," "Angels We Have Heard on High," "We Three Kings of Orient Are," "O Come All Ye Faithful," "Away in a Manger," "Joy to the World," and "Silent Night."

King Herod is sitting on his throne and the Palace Mice are decorating the Christmas tree while the audience sings the first verse of "Deck the Halls." As the song ends, the Palace Mice scamper to the lectern and sit on the floor looking up at the Head Palace Mouse as he/she speaks.

Head Palace Mouse: It is with great joy that I accept your confidence in me as Head Palace Mouse. My family is getting settled here in our new home, and I must say we are pleased. This palace has everything! It is far superior to any other palace in Jerusalem. Sharing the facilities with King Herod and his family has its ups and downs, but I am sure we will manage.

(Pointing to the back)

Wait a minute. Who are those strangers outside the palace? They must be newcomers to Jerusalem. Hmmm. I better send out some mice to find out who they are *(beckoning to Palace Mice)* Palace Mice! Find out who those strangers are.

(Palace Mice scamper to the back where the Magi and the Head Magi are waiting.)

Song: "We Three Kings"

(During the singing of "We Three Kings," the Palace Mice lead the Magi and Head Magi Mouse slowly up the aisle where they stand in front of Herod's throne. The Palace Mice return to the lectern and sit in front of it.)

Head Palace Mouse: Hello! Hello! Excuse me. You seem to be new to these parts. Who are you? What are you looking for? Why are you here in Jerusalem?

Head Magi Mouse: Are you speaking to me?

Head Palace Mouse: Yes. I am. Who *are* you?

Head Magi Mouse: I am a mouse.

Head Palace Mouse: I can see that. But you're not from around here. What tribe are you from?

Head Magi Mouse: I am the Head Magi Mouse. I live with the Magi. They are wise and learned people. We are following the star.

Head Palace Mouse: But why have you come to Herod's Palace?

Head Magi Mouse: We are searching for the new baby who is going to be the King of the Jews.

Head Palace Mouse: A new baby is going to be the King of the Jews? I'm not sure Herod will like this. He thinks *he* is the king of the Jews. And you say a new king is soon to be born? I smell trouble brewing.

(*King Herod has been grumbling and listening to this dialogue and becoming increasingly angry. Then he has an idea. He stands up, smiles and holds out his arms as if to welcome the people to his palace.*)

Head Palace Mouse (*interpreting Herod's miming gestures*): What? No kidding! A dinner party? Right here in this palace? Wow! That's great! And everybody is invited. Even the magi. That's even better. I've got to gather all the Palace Mice. The pickings are going to be awesome. If our poor country cousins had any idea!

(*All sit and the Head Field Mouse jumps up to the pulpit.*)

Head Field Mouse: Hi. Someone call me? I keep hearing these strange sounds. It's usually so quiet in the fields at night. That's why I love being a field mouse. The shepherds are always so generous. They share their food with us. And the sheep even let us have pieces of wool to line our nests!

The city critters wonder what we do for entertainment out here in the country. But they have no idea what it's like to sit around the campfire at night with the shepherds and listen to the jokes and the laughter. But wait a minute! There is something strange in the air tonight. Don't you feel it? Listen. I hear something.

Song: "It Came Upon the Midnight Clear"

(*As the stanza is sung, the Angels stand up on their chairs or risers. The Shepherds walk slowly up the aisle to the front where they sit on the floor looking up at the Angels.*)

Head Field Mouse: There's something special about this night. I can just feel it. I think we had better have a country council meeting and check this out. Field mice! Country Mice! Deer Mice!

(*The Field Mice begin scampering from the back of the church or meeting room. Some of them crawl under the pews—with electrifying effects! When they get to the front they sit with the Shepherds. While the Field Mice are "scampering," the Head Field Mouse continues speaking.*)

We are having a mouse meeting and you are all invited. Check with the shepherds on your way to the meeting place and see if you can gather any news.

Song: "While Shepherds Watched Their Flocks by Night"

(*During the song the Angels, who have been standing on their chairs, lift their arms towards the Shepherds in the form of a blessing.*)

Head Field Mouse: I knew there was going to be something different about this night. Angels! Real angels! Did you hear what they said? "Fear not: for behold, I bring you good tidings of great joy, which shall be to all people. For unto you is born this day in the city of David, a Savior, which is Christ the Lord. And this shall be a sign unto you; you shall find the babe wrapped in swaddling clothes, lying in a manger."

Song: "Angels We Have Heard On High"

(*At song's end, Angels sit down.*)

Head Field Mouse: "Let us now go even unto Bethlehem, and see this thing which has come to pass, which the Lord has made known unto us."

(*Head Field Mouse leads Shepherds and Field Mice down the aisle to the back.*)

Palace Mouse (*at lectern*): What a feast! And King Herod still didn't get what he was after. The scribes and priests had no idea where this new king of the Jews could be found. And so the next day Herod invited the magi to his palace and said to them . . .

(*Herod stands and mimes*)

"Go to Bethlehem and make a careful search for the child; and when you find him, let me know, so that I too may go and worship him."

When the wise men left the palace the huge bright star that has been in the sky the last few nights was still shining bright and sparkly. The wise men seem to be following it. Maybe we should go with them.

Song: Chorus Of "We Three Kings"

(During the song, the Palace Mouse leads the Magi, the Head Magi, and the Palace Mice slowly down the center aisle to the back. Herod, meanwhile, quietly exits.)

Stable Mouse (*running up to the pulpit from the back*): Wow! Did you hear the news? I'm so excited I can't stand still. Everyone is coming here to Bethlehem. The streets are going to be packed with people. Where there's people, there's food. And where there's food . . . (*rubs his stomach*) But let me introduce myself. I am the Stable Mouse and I live here in these stables. I used to live in the inn over there. They have lots of people that live there and, as you know, where there's people, there's food! It was paradise . . . Until—the innkeeper got a cat! That's when I realized it was time for me to get lost. There was no room in the inn.

(Joseph, who has been sitting in the front row, now walks slowly to the back. He stops frequently to mime—pleading for a room.)

So I moved out here to the stable. Not many *people* come out here, but I've made friends with all the animals. We work together and eat together and everyone is happy. Do you know the nicest thing about living in a stable? No one ever complains about not having enough room. There's always room for one more. Speaking of which—who is that?

(Stable Mouse moves to center front, watches Joseph for a moment, and then calls . . .)

Joseph! Joseph!! You can stay here. Honest, we've got lots of room!!!

(Joseph doesn't seem to hear and continues moving to the back of the playing area. Stable Mouse returns to the pulpit.)

Don't get discouraged, Joseph. You can stay here. Bring Mary with you. The animals will keep you warm.

(Head Field Mouse and Head Palace Mouse enter from back and start scampering up the aisle.)

He doesn't hear me. We've got to help them. (*Spotting the mice*) Who are you? You look like the Palace Mouse from King Herod's palace in Jerusalem. And *you* look like the Field Mouse that lives with the shepherds.

Do you want to help? Sure you can help. Go and bring Mary and Joseph here. They can't find any room in the inn, but we can keep them warm and comfortable out here. Oh yes, and bring the magi and shepherds, too. Mary and Joseph are going to have a little baby. It's time for all of us to celebrate!

Song: "O Come All Ye Faithful"

(*During the song, all the actors come up to the front and stand in a semi-circle. A stool and a manger are brought in for Mary, Joseph and the Baby*).

Song: "Away In a Manger"

(*Mary, Joseph and the Baby walk slowly to the front, led by the Head Field Mouse and the Head Palace Mouse.*)

Song: "Joy to the World"

Song: "Silent Night"

Field Mouse: I am only a little field mouse, but Jesus has made me important.

Palace Mouse: I may be a palace mouse, but Jesus taught me the true meaning of humility.

Stable Mouse: As the stable mouse I was as close to Jesus as any one. But now I know the real secret of the gospel.

Field Mouse: We're all close to Jesus!

Palace Mouse: And Jesus is close to us all.

Stable Mouse: May his spirit be with you this Christmas, and may God's love never let you go.

All Three Mice: Amen!!!

Four Musicals

(1) Godspell

Godspell is a soft rock musical based on the Gospel according to St. Matthew. The show was conceived and originally directed by John-Michael Tebelak, with Stephen Schwartz supplying the music. *Godspell* opened in the summer of 1971 in the Off-Broadway Promenade Theatre in New York. It has been playing around the world ever since in schools, theaters, and churches.

Google "Playbill's Highlights from Stephen Schwartz's *Godspell*" for an indication of how extraordinarily lively this show can be. Amateurs, however, may find the libretto sketchy at points. Our unofficial guidebook *Spotlight on Godspell* attempts to address this challenge (www.spotlighton-godspell.com).

Religious critics sometimes claim that *Godspell* mocks Jesus with its colorful costumes, rock music, and witty dialogue. This is wildly unfair. Granted, *Godspell* tells the gospel story with astonishing humor and energy. The story itself, however, is never twisted out of shape. The real heretics, one suspects, are the people who make Jesus out to be a pious bore.

For information concerning *Godspell* scripts and production rights, contact Theatre Maximus at nvpdanan@aol.com or Music Theatre International in New York; London, England; or Melbourne, Australia.

(2) Joseph and the Amazing Technicolor Dreamcoat

Hated by his jealous brothers and sold as a slave into Egypt, Joseph nevertheless ends up interpreting the Pharoah's dreams and becoming the king's right-hand man. His brothers, meanwhile, back in the land of Canaan, suffer endless famines. They are finally forced to reach out to the Egyptian authorities for help. The "helper" turns out to be their long lost brother who reveals himself now in a gospel-anticipating act of mercy and grace.

The music in *Joseph* never stops. It includes disco ("Go, Go, Go Joseph"), country ("One More Angel in Heaven"), calypso ("Benjamin Calypso"), rock ("Song of the King"), ballad ("Close Every Door") and other genres. The show began as a fifteen minute play for a school assembly (lyrics by Tim Rice, music by, note the name, Andrew Lloyd Webber) and kept expanding until it became a world famous musical.

Our own modest production in Huntsville, Ontario was performed, as almost all of our shows are, in the round. The audience was seated on risers surrounding three quarters of the playing area. The children forming the chorus sat on the floor at the feet of the audience while the teenagers and adults in the cast kicked up their heels and sang and danced non-stop. A more energetic show, short of *Godspell*, is hard to imagine.

Contact The Musical Company (info@themusicalcompany.com) for scripts and performance rights.

(3) *Footloose*

This dance-crazed show boasts a compelling story line and such remarkably upbeat and melodious songs as "Let's Hear It for the Boys," "Holding Out for a Hero," "The Girl Gets Around," and "Dancing Is Not a Crime."

Footloose entertains, but it also raises an important moral question. Does the Christian ethic encourage a pro-fun approach to life or does it represent, as Nietzsche and others have long claimed, a kill-joy ethic that essentially robs life of happiness and joy?

The question is poignantly raised when four teenagers from a small Midwestern town have too much boozy fun at a dance one night, and are killed in a car accident on the way home. The father of one of the boys, a preacher by trade, manages to outlaw dancing in the town in the hope of preventing such a tragedy from ever happening again.

Enter Ren, the new kid in town with a long-time passion for dance, and a developing passion for the preacher's daughter. Tensions mount, positions harden, and the story reaches a climax at a Town Council meeting where Ren cites some surprisingly pro-dance Bible passages that his girlfriend has marked for him. The biblical passages calm the preacher down, and the show concludes with everyone letting loose on the dance floor.

For scripts and performance rights contact Rodgers and Hammerstein at: editor@rnh.com.

(4) *Anne of Green Gables*

Based on Lucy Maud Montgomery's 1908 novel, the musical *Anne of Green Gables* has been running every summer since 1965 at the Confederation Theatre in Prince Edward Island. (The last time my wife and I were there, the couple sitting beside us had flown in from Tokyo to see the show.)

The story concerns a red-haired, freckle-faced orphan who is adopted by bachelor Matthew Cuthbert and his spinster sister Marilla. However, no sooner does Anne arrive at the Cuthbert farm house than she is told that a mistake has been made, and she must return to the orphanage. Marilla's argument is sound enough: They clearly requested a boy to relieve Matthew, who has a weak heart, from the strenuous chores of the farm. Matthew, however, is the first to intercede on Anne's behalf. Marilla finally gives in; the girl stays; and Matthew's heart—breaks. Our hearts may break too, but not before the dying Matthew voices a sentiment truly heartbreaking in its wistful yearnings for the fleeting joys of childhood:

> "Anne of Green Gables, never change.
> We like you just this way.
> Anne of Green Gables, sweet and strange,
> Stay as you are today."

Google Samuel French Ltd. (info@samuelfrench.com) for script and performance rights of the original musical as adapted by Donald Harron from the novel *Anne of Green Gables*, and music by Norman Campbell and others.

Pictures of Theater-in-the-Round

Here are two pictures of plays that Trinity United Church (Huntsville, Ontario) has produced in the round: the comedy *Absent Friends* (above) and the musical *Godspell* (below). More will be said in a moment about the advantages of the round. Simply know that no other form of theater in our experience brings the audience so close to the action on the stage, or gives such a three-dimensional view of that action.

Four Plays By Alan Ayckbourn

Alan Ayckbourn is widely regarded as a comed\ic genius in the theater world today. Funny, yes, and yet the British playwright's work can be easily ruined if his material is played for laughs. Play Ayckbourn for the truth, however, and the laughs come as well. Google the BBC Thames Production of Ayckbourn's *The Norman Conquests* for an illustration of how this paradox plays out on the stage.

Another interesting thing about Ayckbourn is that he prefers to mount his plays in the round, thereby creating a delicious intimacy and feeling of naturalness. Theater in the round is also a lot easier on the pocketbook. Just arrange a few risers in a circle or semi-circle, hang some stage lights, douse the house lights, and presto, everyone in the audience has a bird's eye view of the action.

Here are some of Ayckbourn's most popular and easy-to-produce plays. Scripts and performance rights available through Samuel French (info@samuelfrench.com).

(1) *The Norman Conquests*

The Norman Conquests actually consists of three plays: *Table Manner*s is set in the dining room, *Living Together* in the living room, and *Round and Round the Garden* in the garden. The same six characters appear in each play.

Domestic shenanigans abound as Annie agrees to spend an illicit weekend with her sister Ruth's husband Norman only to have her plans foiled by Annie's older brother Reg and his overbearing wife Sarah.

The first thing Sarah does is summon Ruth to check up on her straying husband. Sarah then attempts to jolt Annie's feckless boyfriend Tom, the local vet, into action. Alas, Tom, being Tom, remains oblivious to almost everything going on around him.

And Norman? Perhaps Norman's wife Ruth describes him best, saying at one point, "It's a bit like owning an oversized unmanageable dog, being married to Norman. He's not very well house-trained, he needs continual exercises—and it's sensible to lock him up if you have visitors . . . But I'd hate to get rid of him."

Alan Ayckbourn has written over 75 plays. *The Norman Conquests* may well be the most entertaining of them all.

(2) *Time of My Life*

Gerry Stratton, a successful business man, has organized a small family dinner with his wife and sons, and their significant others. At one point, son Glyn is alone with his wife Stephanie, the others having left the restaurant. Glyn has just informed Steph that he is leaving her and the kids for Sarah. A painful decision, for sure, but Glyn wants to make it as manageable as he can. In fact, he plans to give Stephanie ample financial help, even the car.

"Don't bother about the bill," Glyn says at last. "I'll . . . You've been amazing, Steph. Absolutely amazing over all this. Thank you. I mean it. I won't forget it. Thank you."

Glyn now leaves the restaurant, and Stephanie is left by herself only to have Tuto, the waiter, come bouncing in with dessert suggestions: "You want a sweet? What you like? We have the specialties. Smooliboos. That is cream with meringue?" Stephanie mechanically nods.

On and on Tuto rolls: "You like that? You want something with it? Some delicious tickletasse? This is delicious tart with treacle and cream mixed with passion fruit, fresh strawberries and Armagnac . . ." Stephanie just sits there, nodding and quietly sobbing.

Audiences don't know whether to laugh or cry.

(3) *Woman in Mind*

Woman in Mind finds Ayckbourn dramatizing one of the greatest problems in churches today: boring clerics. Okay, I may be one of them. But even I am not as bad as the vicar in this play. Gerald is writing a 60 page history of his parish, and driving his wife crazy (literally) almost every time he opens his mouth.

Susan finally decides to cope by conjuring up a fantasy family that consists of an ideal daughter (Lucy), a perfect husband (Andy), and a charming brother-in-law (Tony). This dream family nicely takes care of Susan's problems until they are torn from her fantasizing mind and replaced by her all too real and grim sister-in-law (Muriel), her religiously fanatical son (Rick), and of course by Gerald.

The play ends with Susan slipping away entirely from reality into a delusory state that finds her conflating both the real and the ideal family in a thank you speech that is appropriately nonsensical: "Dearest friends. Family. My happiest moment has been to stand here with you all and share this, my most precious of days. I grow hugh, summer few bald teddy know these two wonderful children, Lucy and Rick. I cannot tell you how heaply cowed siam . . ."

Again, Ayckbourn leaves audiences hardly knowing whether to laugh or cry.

(4) *Absent Friends*

This is one of Ayckbourn's saddest plays, and yet also one of his funniest as the play repeatedly throws light on the double-edged nature of life. Life is beautiful and yet often challenging beyond words.

This paradox is dramatized in *Absent Friends* at a tea party that Colin's friends have arranged in order to comfort him over the recent death of his fiancée. Colin is absent at the beginning of the play which gives his friends time to reveal their true emotions about death. When Colin finally arrives, there is no question that he is the strongest person in the room while all the others, so full of themselves on the outside, are nervous wrecks within.

The "friends" include Marge, a scatterbrained shopaholic; Evelyn, a gum-chewing adulteress; Paul, a chauvinistic adulterer; John, a restless jigger trying to make an extra buck; and Diana, an uptight hostess on the way to a nervous breakdown. And then of course there's Colin whose inner peace in the face of death rattles the others to the depths of their being.

A Children's Play by Alan Ayckbourn

Ernie's Incredible Illucinations

ILLUCINATIONS IS A LITTLE one act giggle of a play dealing with the imaginary ramblings of one incorrigible kid called Ernie. This is unquestionably Ayckbourn's most beloved children's play, a favorite with both casts and audiences.

What a character Ernie is! A real day dreamer whose dreams keep turning into reality. Everywhere he goes, Ernie causes Nazi soldiers to appear, championship boxing aunties to enter the ring, mountain climbing rescues to take place in the local library. In short, the lad is a walking nightmare. So Mum and Dad take Ernie to a most sceptical doctor who concocts a most astonishing diagnosis.

Ernie's Incredible Illucinations is an ideal play for the few kids who want something to sink their teeth into, and the many who are just happy to be around for the fun.

An easy play to produce and a popular one with audiences of every age. Again, as with all of Ayckbourn plays, *Ernie's Incredible Illucinations* is available through Samuel French.

3

Music

Liturgical Responses

Touch Me Again, Lord

Touch me again Lord, touch me again, Lord

With healing hands thy grace impart.

Touch me again Lord, speak to my soul, Lord,

Heal all my being, my mind and my heart.

—E. R. GREENWOOD

E. R. GREENWOOD IS a gifted composer and lyricist with an evangelical soul. The Greenwoods came to Canada from England one year to visit their daughter who happened to live near us. One evening we invited the family to our home for dinner. After the meal we adjourned to the living room, and Mr. Greenwood, noticing our piano, offered to play a few of his religious compositions. I was polite, but not exactly hopeful. Soon, however, Ted Greenwood's soft, warm, melodic music was washing over me, and I realized that a very fine composer had just graced my little world.

"Touch Me Again, Lord" is one of E.R. Greenwood's liturgical pieces: a beautiful sung response following the prayer of confession and moment of silence.

Touch Me Again Lord

E.R. Greenwood

Gloria Patri

Glory be to the Father,
And to the Son, and to the Holy Spirit;
As it was in the beginning,
Is now, and ever shall be,
World without end.
Amen. Amen.

—*ADAPTED FOR SINGING BY JOHN WEAVER*

John Weaver's "Gloria Patri" is one of the finest Glorias that I have ever come across. Tuneful, strong, melodious, it works especially well in the context of the Lord's Supper.

The composer served as organist and director of Music at the Madison Avenue Presbyterian Church in New York from 1970–2005. Weaver's "Gloria Patri" was originally published in *Reformed Liturgy & Music* (Volume XV111, Winter, 1984).

Gloria Patri

Stay with Us through the Night

Words: Walter Farquharson

Music: Ron Klusmeier

The opening stanza of Walter Farquharson and Ron Klusmeier's hymn "Stay with Us through the Night" offers worshippers a fine sung benediction that can follow the worship leader's spoken benediction.

The words of the chorus—"Stay with us through the night. Stay with us through the pain. Stay with us blessed stranger, till the morning breaks again."—recall the time two disciples of the Lord encountered a stranger on their way to a village called Emmaus. As the two men walked along the road with the stranger, they discussed the amazing things that had recently happened. Finally, they stopped to break bread together, but the stranger made as if to continue his journey. The others, however, pressed him to stay with them: "for evening draws on, and the day is almost over."

Later, as the stranger broke bread with them, their eyes were opened, and they recognised him only to have him vanish from their sight (Luke 24:13–32). Thus this concluding chorus in the worship service reminds us that we do not walk into the new week alone: the crucified and risen "stranger" walks with us.

Sing this opening stanza as a chorus or postlude for a couple Sundays in a row and people may like it well enough. Sing it for three months or so, and people may very well become wedded to the piece.

Stay with Us through the Night

Words: Walter Farqubarson
Music: Rom Klusmeier

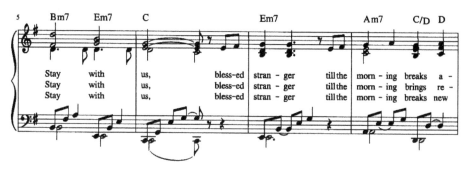

A New Christmas Carol

Only a Baby

> *"Only a baby just a little boy,*
> *And yet the sky is shining with love.*
> *Lying small and helpless in his mother's arms*
> *Can he see the star up above?"*

—*Music by Barbara Beattie and Bryan Buchan*

—*Lyrics by Bryan Buchan*

—*Arrangement by Chris Buchan*

Two hundred years ago, just before Christmas, a young priest in a village near Salzburg learned that the organ in his church had broken down. The priest asked an organist in a nearby town to compose a melody that the priest could use with a guitar while he sang the words of a Christmas hymn that he had recently written.

Thus "Silent Night" was born.

Forty years ago, Bryan Buchan and Barbara Beattie, members of St. Matthew's United Church in Richmond Hill, Ontario, composed a Christmas carol for a Cantata that they were writing together. The Cantata was appreciated by the congregation, but then it sunk out of sight, taking "Only a Baby" with it.

The carol, however, stayed with me. Every Christmas, "Only a Baby" plays in my head. I know this piece is good. As good as any Christmas carol. Perhaps even as good as "Silent Night".

It only needs to be discovered.

Only a Baby

Music: Barbara Beattie & Bryan Buchan
Lyrics: Bryan Buchan
Arrangement: Chris Buchan

1.On-ly a ba-by just a lit-tle boy, And yet the sky is shin-ing with love.
3.On-ly a ba-by just a lit-tle boy, A boy who brings us kings from a - far.

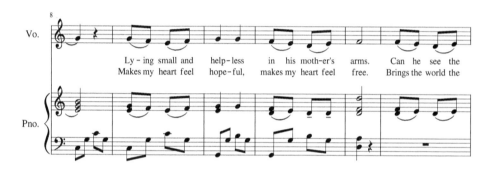

Ly - ing small and help-less in his moth-er's arms. Can he see the
Makes my heart feel hope-ful, makes my heart feel free. Brings the world the

star up a - bove? 2.On-ly a boy. He's just a lit-tle child. They say he's born to
light of his star.

Fine

Fm

rule ov-er all. But can he real-ly free us and bring us peace and hope. A baby is so

ve — ry small.

4

Hymns

Hymns Old and New

(1) "For All the Saints"

THE 20TH CENTURY BRITISH composer Ralph Vaughan Williams provided the music for the 19th century writer William Walsham How's hymn, "For All the Saints, who from their labours rest, all who by faith before the world confessed, your name, O Jesus, be forever blest. Hallelujah, hallelujah!" Choirs especially will enjoy Williams' magnificent harmonies in this hymn.

(2) "O World of God"

The lyrics of this hymn by the Old Testament scholar R. B. Y. Scott transform the words of William Blake's nationalistic hymn *Jerusalem* into a far more theologically insightful, and yet still poetically charming piece. There was never anything wrong with Hubert Parry's majestic tune *Jerusalem*. However, we now have great lyrics to accompany it.

(3) "Abide with Me"

I love this old chestnut. Okay, maybe I'm the only person today who still loves it. But, no, google Mary Jess Leaverland's rendition of the hymn as sung at the outset of Britain's 2012 FA Final, and one quickly realizes that if the children of light aren't particularly enamored with this hymn the children of the world still get it. This glorious hymn just needs to be sung and not moaned.

(4) *"Halle, Halle, Halle"*

This traditional liturgical text was re-arranged by the Iona Community in 1990. The word "Halle" is an abbreviation of "Hallelujah" meaning, "Praise Yahweh," which is to say "Praise God." Clap, dance, jiggle your arms, throw your whole body and soul into this wonderfully infectious chorus.

(5) *"River in Judea"*

Jack Feldman's gospel anthem is a huge favorite with massed choirs. Google the Dorian 07 Summer Camp's rendition of this hymn to gain a sense of its rousing grandeur.

(6) *"Laudate Dominum"*

Google Askel Rykkvin's performance of Mozart's "Laudate Dominum" for an especially beautiful rendition of this heavenly anthem. The music itself was composed just before Wolfgang, at the age of 25, finally broke the apron strings in Salzburg and headed out for the glamor and opportunity of Vienna. Can an average church choir today sing this hymn? Of course it can. It can also, incidentally, sing Mozart's heavenly "Ave Verum Corpus."

(7) *"Silent Spring"*

"Silent Spring" is a grim but necessary reminder that climate change is no liberal fad but one of the most pressing and serious issues of our day. Words by New Zealand's Shirley Erena Murray, music by Canada's incomparable Ron Klusmeier:

> *"Now is the time for a reckoning,*
> *Now all is flowery and flourishing,*
> *God, help your children mindfully listen:*
> *Soon there may be just a silent spring*
> *Silent spring, silent spring."*

(8) *"Before the Marvel of This Night"*

Google the Baylor A Cappella Choir's rendition of "Before the Marvel of This Night" to realize just how lovely this new Christmas carol is. The American Lutheran Carl F. Schalk gave us the music, Jaroslav J. Vajda the words. Schalk and Vajda, incidentally, also gave us the exquisitely beautiful children's hymn, "God of the Sparrow."

(9) *"In the Bulb There Is a Flower"*

This hymn by Natalie Sleeth was originally a choral anthem. Soon after the anthem was composed, Mrs. Sleeth's husband was diagnosed with cancer. When Mr. Sleeth died, the anthem, at his request, was sung at his funeral. (Natalie Sleeth did not permit any of her other songs to be sung on that occasion.) The choral anthem, however, made such a strong impression on the mourners that word spread and the anthem soon became a widely used and much beloved hymn.

(10) *"The Lord Is My Shepherd"*

Dozens of arrangements are available for "The Lord is My Shepherd." One of the most melodious is surely the one that Howard Goodall composed, and is used as an introduction to the popular BBC TV series, "The Vicar of Dibley." You Tube performances of this anthem worth checking out include those identified as Morgwyn 21, Maestroz 25, and the Georgia Boy Choir.

(11) *"Turn Your Eyes Upon Jesus"*

This simple, evangelical chorus goes straight to the soul both in terms of the words and the music. Google Elvis Presley's YouTube rendition to realize just how beautiful this chorus is. There's an old saying, "Why should the devil have all the best tunes?" By the same token we might ask, "Why should mainliners have all the best hymns?" Here's one from our evangelical friends that is surely well worth rediscovering.

A Note on Acoustics

For music to be good, it is not enough for it to be good. It also has to be heard. And nothing mitigates more powerfully against *hearing* music in churches than carpet.

Granted, carpet adds a touch of color and warmth. But at a terrible price in terms of muffling sound. This is why, of course, one rarely sees carpet on the stages of concert halls. The children of the world know that carpet acts like an acoustical wet blanket soaking up the sounds of lively song and music. Why can't the children of light learn this lesson as well? Chalk it up to stubbornness, I suppose. Carpet looks nice and we're used to it, so why change? That seems to be our thinking.

I remember the struggle we had convincing our own congregation on this score. Finally, we borrowed a number of four by eight sheets of plywood from the local lumber yard, and covered the chancel floor with the plywood. Just for one Sunday.

That, however, was enough for the congregation to notice a dramatic improvement in sound. Finally, people could make out the words of the choir! Finally, the congregation could hear *itself* singing! We soon received congregational approval to rip up the carpet in the chancel (leaving a harmless strip in the aisle). We then sanded and varnished the floor, and never looked back. Carpet bedrooms, not churches!

A Note on Presentation

Choristers might well give some thought, not only to the content, but to the way in which they present their music. Normally a choir stands up, sings the song, and sits down. And that's about it.

Nothing wrong with that. But does it always have to be done that way?

Why not encourage the choir sometimes to encircle the whole congregation or audience. Or sing from the back of the hall. Or have a soloist sing from the back while the rest remain at the front. Or simply have everybody gather around the piano.

Even more boldly, why not work a little choreography into the number! Google, for example, the National Taiwan University Choir's super-dynamic presentation of "We Go Together" from the Broadway musical *Grease*. Here we have young college students from Taiwan of all places taking a song that is as American as apple pie, and instead of saying, as so many of us might be tempted to say, "Don't like it; never tried it," they end up singing this song in an extraordinarily lively and creative way. It all began surely with a Taiwanese choir director bringing a choreographer to a rehearsal and saying, "Okay, now help us sing this song as if the kids just stepped out of the movie."

5

Prayers

Introducing Judith Brocklehurst and Harold Wells

OUR WORSHIP LEADERS IN this chapter are Judith Brocklehurst and Harold Wells. Judith is gone now, but I remember her well as a delightful if unpredictable parishioner.

One Sunday morning at worship Judith read the Scripture lesson that finds Jesus returning to the synagogue in his home town. Jesus, you may recall, read the passage in Isaiah where the Lord anoints the prophet to bring good news to the poor and deliverance to the captives. When he finished the reading, he sat down "and the eyes of all of them that were in the synagogue, were fastened on him." Finally, Jesus looked up and announced that the scripture had been fulfilled that day in the congregation's hearing.

Judith for her part read the same passage, or at least most of it, and then tossed the Bible across the chancel to yours truly (fortunately I was quick enough to catch it). She then went and sat down on the chancel steps. After a moment of reflection, Judith looked up and delivered the last line of the reading: "Today this scripture has been fulfilled in your hearing."

Harold Wells is also an effective leader of worship. After serving pastorates in Ontario and the African country of Lesotho (where he also taught theology), Harold taught Systematic Theology at Toronto's Emmanuel College for over twenty years.

Prayers for Worship

Opening Prayers

God, eternal Spirit, Creator of all humanity,
of the planet Earth, and the whole universe,
We approach you with awe and wonder
knowing that you are far beyond our comprehension
in light inaccessible.
Yet, in Jesus the Christ you have drawn near to us
in our own human flesh,
and by your Spirit, you live within us.
We praise and adore you in your majesty and glory,
but also in your lowliness and suffering.
Be with us now in a special way,
so that we may worship you with mind and heart,
and hear your Word of truth. In Christ our Lord we pray,
Amen.

—*HAROLD WELLS*

Father, we come here to worship; to say to you that we recognize your gift of life, and are grateful for it. Our living is not easy; it is not easy to live well. So we look to you to lead us onward, through the joy and hurt, the confusion and love, which awaits each and all of us. In Jesus' name. Amen.

—*HAROLD WELLS*

God of all joy, we celebrate before you the exhilaration of summer. We exult in the heat of sandy beaches, cool fresh water, wind in the woods, camp fires at dusk and new-found friends. O Spirit who lives and breathes in all that is beautiful and alive, we praise and worship you! Amen.

—*HAROLD WELLS*

Lord who created us, your glory is infinite, your splendor eclipses that of the stars. The farthest atom, in the depths of space, is not more distant from us, than we are from you. Yet when you call us here to worship, you call us home. We bring our hungry, dirty, empty little souls to you, to be cleansed with words of love and fed with food from heaven. We bring our cramped, overcrowded lives, to be spread out in the light of your radiance. We are set free to rejoice, to sing and laugh and play in the freedom of heaven, the glorious liberty of the children of God. We are called out, to advance from glory to glory; we are called up, to grow into infinite love. What can we do, but praise you and bless you and thank you, Lord who created us. Amen.

—JUDITH BROCKLEHURST

Most Holy One, we do not need to tell you the things we did that we wish we had not done; the things we said that we wish we could unsay; the thoughts and feelings we are ashamed of. You know them all already; you know them, and you love us. We bring them before you now, we bring them before ourselves, because we know that you can help us, our Father, our Mother, our Friend. We cannot deal with these things, but you can. In Jesus' name, we ask you to help us. Amen.

—JUDITH BROCKLEHURST

Well, here we are, God. You've got fifty-eight minutes. But please don't let the preacher bore us. And please not too much of that radical stuff about sin and suffering. Still, we think You ought to get us into the right frame of mind. After all, we are here. We'd like to make the most of it. So, within those limits, God, enlighten us, inspire us, and open our minds and hearts to your everlasting love! We pray with tongue in cheek but with heart, we hope, in the right place. Amen.

—JUDITH BROCKLEHURST

Prayers of Confession

God of grace, Creator and Savior
You know that we are dust,
weak, vulnerable and mortal,
yet, made in your image with potential
for love, for courage, and great achievement.
You know that often we try our best,
that we try to do what is right,
but our love is small, our courage is shaky,
and our achievements far below our potential.
In your gracious love, forgive us again, and accept us
as your beloved children.
Especially today we remember our failure
to care for the earth as we should,
because we prefer our own pleasure and convenience
to the long-term well-being of humanity and other creatures.
Forgive us our sin of short-sightedness and willful blindness.
Renew us and build us up by the indwelling of your Spirit,
We pray in Christ Jesus, our Saviour and Lord. Amen.

—*HAROLD WELLS*

Father, we confess we have thought more of our own achievements than of your love; we have measured our lives by the success we have had rather than by the love we have given; we have forgotten that your Son came to us, not as a master, but as a servant and friend. Help us, Father. Amen.

—*JUDITH BROCKLEHURST*

Dear God, we're sorry this isn't going to be more fun. We really haven't any exciting sins to offer to you this week. All we managed was a little jealousy, a little covetousness, a little nitpicking. Even worse, we didn't get excited about much either. The suffering in the world, the poverty, the misery all just floated by us like an unabsorbed TV commercial. Forgive us, God, for boring you and for being bored with you and your call to action. Amen.

—JUDITH BROCKLEHURST

Prayers of the People

Our gracious Creator God,

we come before you with our concerns for the world,

for ourselves and for others.

By your Spirit dwelling in us,

keep us mindful of those in need,

for those whom we know who are sick or in trouble,

those who are bereaved, or suffering loneliness.

Particularly now we remember . . .

also . . .

We think of our ministers, Alison and Josephine, praying that your Spirit will always be at work in them

as they do their important work among us.

We pray that your Spirit may be at work

inspiring and empowering the environmental and ecological movements

which struggle on behalf of all people and all creatures.

We pray for the animal kingdom, our cousins

in all their energy, beauty, struggle and pain.

We pray for the soil, the seas, the forests, and the vast kingdom of plants

that they may flourish and rejoice in greater health and well being.

And so, as we pray for them, we commit ourselves again,

To live in love and justice,

And in harmony with your wonderful creatures all around us.

We pray in the name of our brother in the flesh, your Son, our Lord, Jesus the Christ. Amen.

—HAROLD WELLS

At the Graveside of a Young Friend

Lord of grace and glory, we thank you for Coral's life. We thank you for giving her to us, her family and her friends. We thank you for her courage and grace, her gaiety, and the love and fun she brought into our lives. We thank you for the great love she and Paul had for one another, that in their distress, they clung to one another in true married love. We thank you that she honored us by enlisting us in her struggle, demanding the utmost of us, bringing us into fellowship with her and with each other, creating love. We thank you that, baptized a Christian, she lived in the fellowship of your church and died in utter peace in the sure hope of everlasting life. Lord, help us as we mourn her death. Help us to grieve, with sadness indeed but without anger or bitterness. Help us, in the face of things we do not understand, to trust your never-failing love. Give us faith to see in death the gate of everlasting life. Help us to know that, when every battle was lost for Coral, you came yourself, and won the last battle, and that she is with you now, in the place of joy and light, where sorrow and pain are no more, but life eternal. Amen

—*JUDITH BROCKLEHURST*

6

Communion

A Communion Service

Prepared by Paul Scott Wilson

THIS COMMUNION LITURGY IS *simply beautiful. I have used it many times.
Indeed, in recent years I have used it exclusively. This is the way Thomas
Cranmer might well have worded his communion service had he lived in the
21st century.*

*Yes, it's an elegantly worded service. But more than that, Paul Wilson's
liturgy trains the spotlight exactly on the One who is glorified as the people
give thanks, the bread is broken and the little cup of grape juice (or wine) is
shared.*

A Communion Liturgy

The Lord be with you.

>*And also with you.*

Lift up your hearts!

>*We lift them up to the Lord.*

Let us give thanks to the Lord our God.

>*It is right to give thanks and praise.*

O God, you launched into the void earth, air, water, light; created out of nothing, in no time, in no place. Your Word went issuing forth into nothing, through space, its rolling form creating form, its passing whirl creating time.

>*Let the universe cry out and magnify your name.*

You planted the dust with gold and iron ore, rich humus and secret springs, and laced the air with light and spore. You creatured the elements with flight and movement, and yarned from the dust seed-laden fruit and ground-nut, root and herb.

>*Let the universe cry out and magnify your name.*

You beckoned us on the not-yet-side of life and fragile forms both fearful and wonderful. Awesome is the swell of the symphony you have shaped; mighty is the movement of our gathered dance.

>*Sung*
>*Holy, holy, holy Lord*
>*God of power and might;*
>*Holy, holy, holy Lord,*
>*God of power and might.*
>*Heav'n and earth are full.*
> *Full of your glory.*
> *Hosanna in the highest, hosanna in the highest.*
> *Blessed is he who comes in the name of the Lord*
> *Hosanna in the highest hosanna in the highest.*

(music from Franz Schubert's Deutsche Messe, *1826, adapt. Richard Proulz)*

But we have stumbled in our dance, and our notes have turned to noise. Yet still you have lightly borne us to our feet to turn and turn and turn again. You came to us, our form a mirror of yours. You ate with the outcast and brought rest to the weary. You healed and spoke in parables, and for a time we were touched by reality.

Let the universe cry out and magnify your name.

But we could not stand in the face of truth, and in time we could stand
you no longer. We crafted cross from tree. As the universe shuddered in
its glide and the tumult of death grew deafening, Jesus gave thanks for the
bread he then broke and offered to the disciples saying, "Take this and eat,
it is my body given for you." He gave thanks for the wine he then poured,
saying, "This is the cup of the new covenant in my blood. Drink of this,
all of you; this is poured out for you and for many." Eating now this bread
and drinking from this cup, we join our brothers and sisters everywhere,
those who have passed this way, and those still to come, and with all creation, witnessing to your life, your victory over death, your presence.

Christ has died. Christ is risen. Christ will come again.

You have splashed us by the play of your waters on our lives and claimed
us as your own; so we come to your table bearing gifts, reclaiming the re-
birth that is our ongoing way. Let your Spirit hover over these gifts as over
the waters at the beginning. Bless them, that we may be united in Christ's
body, in the breaking and in the sharing. Far beyond and outracing us is
the mystery of your tolerance and love, issuing forth again through space,
creating and not returning void. All glory, praise and honour be to you, O
God.

Let the universe cry out and magnify your name.

Sharing of the Elements

> *Post-communion Prayer*
> *Gracious God, to you we offer our heartfelt thanks. You have beck-*
> *oned us to partake of our salvation first in your Word broken open*
> *in preaching, now at your Table and taken into our being. For the*
> *bread of Christ's body, for the wine of his blood, for the unity of his*
> *unending purpose, we give you our thanks. Keep us in the tender-*
> *ness of your abiding love, that we may be broken in the nurture*
> *of others, until we are again here gathered, restored in you, the*
> *unwavering hope of all creation.*
> *Amen.*

7

Dramatic Readings

Advent Readings for Children of All Ages (with a nod to Dr. Seuss)

By Jean Hamilton

Dᴜʀɪɴɢ ᴛʜᴇ Sᴜɴᴅᴀʏs ᴏғ *Advent, worship leaders often like to involve members of the congregation in the lighting of the Advent candles. Jean Hamilton, a member of the United Church of Canada, wrote these Dr. Seuss-like verses as an engaging way of bringing the Advent introductions alive.*

Hope

(First Sunday of Advent)

Voice One: It soon will be Christmas, with snowflakes and bells,
    And turkey and candy, and songs and noels.
    Do you know what it means,
    Do you know what it meant?
    And are you all ready, a hundred per cent?

Voice Two: I know what it means, I do get your drift,
    It means I get millions and zillions of gifts.
    It means Christmas morning right under the tree
    There's all kinds of gifts and they're mostly for me.

Voice One: Oh no you're quite wrong, oh no you're adrift
    That isn't my meaning, that isn't my riff
    It's not about millions and zillions at all,
    It's not about piles of stuff bought at the mall
    There's only one gift and it's really quite small
    It really is tiny, it really is little,
    It's hardly as big as a jot or a tittle.

Voice Two: Just one little gift, and that is the reason?
    Just one little gift for the whole Christmas season?
    That really is awful, that really is bad,
    I guess you just haven't been reading the ads.

Voice One: But wait till I tell you, this news is not sad,
    This news is not awful, this news is not bad.
    This news is the best news that you've ever had
    This news is awesome and happy and glad.
    This gift is a baby, this gift is a boy,
    It's all about love, and it's all about joy.
    It's all about hope and it's all about peace
    This baby is sweeter than Pieces by Reese!
    Now what do you think? Now what do you say?
    Do you think this will be such a bad Christmas day?

Voice Two: That really is awesome, and now I agree,
    This gift is for everyone, not for just me!
    I do get your meaning, I do get your drift
    So let's light a candle to honour the Gift!

(lights candle)

Peace

(Second Sunday of Advent)

Voice One: So this is the season, so Advent is here,
We're all getting ready, the message is clear!
The gifts we're all making,
The cakes we're all baking,
There's no use in faking,
The season is here.

Voice Two: Now wait just a minute,
There's no need to shout,
Are you sure that's what Christmas is really about?
So what about peace, and what about joy,
And what about welcoming Mary's new boy?

Voice One: Let's stop all our rushing and think about peace,
And two thousand years hoping conflicts will cease.
The noise all around us is all about war,
And killing and bombing, as bad as before.
So tell me, please tell me, I hope you are able:
Just what is the message that comes from the stable?

Voice Two: You first must be quiet, before you can hear
The sound of the picture, the folks gathered near.
The shepherds and wise men,
The dog and the cat,
The mouse in the corner,
The donkey and rat,
Forgetting their differences,
Forgetting their wrongs
All quiet together,
All getting along,
All hearing the angels,
All hearing their song.
For peaceful means loving,
And this is the thing:
You have to be quiet
To hear angels sing.

Voice One: So let's light a candle,
  A flickering thing
  To remind us to listen
  The angels still sing.

  (lights candle)

Joy

(Third Sunday of Advent)

Voice One: Today is for joy, because Christmas is near.
Do you know what that means? Do you have it quite clear?

Voice Two: Of course, it just means that we're smiling and happy
  And playing
  And singing
  And dancing
  And clappy.

  It really is easy, it's really a cinch, and if you don't get it, you're
likely a grinch!

Voice One: So that is the answer, so that's how it's done?
  It's really as simple as just having fun?

Voice Two: You sound kind of doubtful! Do you think there is more?
  Do you think there's something else Christmas is for?

Voice One: I think fun is great, but I think joy is deeper.
  Like fun comes and goes, but joy is a keeper.
  I think joy's a mystery, richer by far,
  And it all has to do with a stall and a star.
  I think that at Christmas it's there in the air,
  And spreads from the manger to shine everywhere.
  I don't understand it, I just know it's there.

Voice Two: I know you are right, if I just stop and think,
   Joy is the mystery, and love is the link.
   So let's light a candle, for love and for joy
   So we will remember the birth of a boy.

(lights candle)

Love

(Fourth Sunday of Advent)

Voice One: Well, it's Christmas weekend,
   And this is the payoff
   The end of the year and we're into the playoffs!
   For this is the Sunday
   When love is the theme!
   So what do you make of it?
   What is your dream?

Voice Two: I know about love,
   I know all about it
   The singers all sing it
   The shouters all shout it.
   Everyone's shopping
   Wanting to try it,
   Everyone's hopping
   To find it or buy it.
   Just buy the right presents,
   Just drive the right car,
   And love will be yours,
   It's right there in the stars.

Voice One: I think that's a problem,
   I think that's all wrong,
   If that is the story
   You heard in a song.
   It's not about money,

It's not about shopping,
It's not about buying,
It's not about hopping.
Don't have to be pretty,
Don't have to be clever,
Don't have to be anything different whatever.
To love everybody, both neighbor and stranger,
This is the gift of the Child in the manger.

Voice Two: That sounds really cool, I think that I get it.
    Let's light a candle so we never forget it.

(*lights candle*)

A Christmas Eve Choral Reading

Anonymous

Here is a fun *choral reading for the Christmas Eve service. Vary the volume, stretch and contract the words, feel the poetry in it all.*

"Moo!" said the Cow
"Ding-a-dong!" said the Bell;
"Brrrrr!" said the Shepherds as the chill night fell.

"Tax!" said Cyrenius the Governor of Syria;
"Gifts!" said the Kings—gold, frankincense and myrrh;
"Full!" said the landlord—take them to the stable.
"Let him sleep," said Mary, for the world has yet to stir."

"Myrrh" said the Kings
"Ding-a-dong!" said the Bell;
"Peace!" said the Shepherds as the soft snow fell.

"Moo!" said the Cow;
"Ding-a-dong!" said the Bell;
"Joy!" said the Shepherds as the starlight fell.

"Death!" said King Herod to the children of Jerusalem;
"Life!" said the Throng—it sang for Jesus' sake;

"Here!" said the Starlight—guide them to the stable.
"Let him sleep," said Joseph, "for the world is not awake."

"Guide!" said the Star,
"Ding-a-dong!" said the Bell;
(softly) "Gentle," said the Shepherds as the still night fell.
(very softly) "Gentle," said the Shepherds "is our Lord Emmanuel."

A Gospel Reading for Children of All Ages

By Ann Weems

AN ELDERLY WOMAN IN our congregation suffers terribly from arthritis. Bernice can walk, but just barely. Yet one night at a congregational funfest I looked up and there she was dancing. No, not dancing: jiving! The music was rocking, and so was our arthritic-challenged friend. Invite individuals in your group to read selections from this poem and then follow their reading with a little dance of their own. (Piano accompaniment desirable.) Then invite the whole class or congregation to join in singing Sydney Carter's super-energetic hymn, "I Danced in the Morning."

Lord of the Dance

When they ask what happened here,
We'll simply say
Christ came by and we learned his dance.

The Lord does his dance on the temple floor
And the Pharisees are properly shocked:
A mad man,
Dangerous,
Unfit to guide our youth,
A heretic!
And they flee to the public
Where their praying can be seen.

The Lord does his dance with a tax collector
And the Sadducees scream: Now!
Now do you see who he is? He dines with sinners
While we—we have all this work to do.
The man's a winebibber!

The Lord does his dance with a woman of the streets
And the church people rub their hands together gleefully.
Aha! Now we've got you!

But he looked into them
And they crept away,
Unable to throw the first stone.

The Lord does his dance with all the wrong people:
With slaves and lepers and tax collectors,
With cursing fishermen and adulterers and thieves,
With outcasts and castoffs.
He dances with the unclean, with the orphan, with the displaced,
      with the unwhole.
And he won't dance with us
Until we become
(Of all things)
As little children;
Until we admit we are the needy,
     we are the outcasts,
     we are the orphans.
Then he says to us:
     Come unto me!
     And we become the accepted unacceptable,
     Our brokenness is bound,
     And we are able to follow the dance.
The music is never-ending
And if we miss a step or two,
Or if we fall exhausted,
The Lord is always there to pull us to our feet.

So come now, let's dance in the temple!
Let's dance in the city!
Let's dance in the sanctuary and in the streets!
Let's join hands and dance where
The music leads us,
For the Lord's dance is never ending;
The music goes on forever!

The Good Samaritan: Echo Style

By Richard Coleman

RICHARD COLEMAN, THE AUTHOR of Gospel Telling: The Art and Theology of Children's Sermons, *introduces this participatory retelling of the Good Samaritan parable accordingly: "One day Jesus was tested with this question: 'If I am supposed to love my neighbor as myself, who is my neighbor?' Jesus answered by telling a story—this story. I invite you to join me by being an echo, repeating the same words, and performing the same actions after me."*

I am who I am (point to yourself).
One day I put on my sandals (pretend to put on sandals),
And my traveling cloak (mimic slipping arms into loose cloak).
I took my money bag (hold imaginary bag in fist),
And hid it in my belt (mimic tucking it in wide belt).
Then I started on my way (walk in place)
From Jerusalem to Jericho (sweep arm in wide arc),
Uphill and downhill (walk on the spot, leaning backward and then forward),
Past dark caves where robbers might hide (look fearful).
I pretended I wasn't afraid (stand straight, hands clasped behind back);
But all of a sudden I was surrounded by robbers (arms go up),
And one of them hit me (crouch down, hands in front of face to ward off blows);
That was the last thing I remember (bend down even further)
After a while (cup hand to ear)
I heard footsteps (cross arms, slap hands on arms)
The footsteps grew louder (slap more loudly).
It was a priest (stop slapping; hold arms akimbo).
He said, "Can't stop now sonny" (look down and shake head),
But I'll come back later (wave good-bye).
After a while (cup hand to ear),
I heard new footsteps (raise hands to shoulder level; snap fingers).
It was a Levite (continue snapping fingers).
He said, "Too bad, too bad" (shake head);
Then he went on his way (wave good-bye).
Soon I heard other footsteps (slap thighs, one after the other).
It was a Samaritan on a donkey (continue thigh-slapping).

"Whoa! Need any help?" (mimic pulling in reins, lean over and look down);
Then he jumped down (jump up and down once),
And took off his cloak (mimic taking off cloak),
Tore it into strips (pretend to tear strips of cloth),
And bandaged my wounds (mimic rolling bandages on wounded areas).
He lifted me onto his donkey (mimic lifting and placing body gently),
And slowly we went on our way (slap thighs more slowly),
Until we came to an inn (mimic pulling back on reins).
He carried me inside (arms outstretched in carrying position),
And laid me on a bed (pretend to place body on bed).
"Here is some money" he said to the innkeeper (mimic taking coins from bag);
"I will pay all that is owed." (pretend to tuck money bag back in belt).
Then he went on his way (slap thighs).
Now I ask you (point finger at listeners),
Which one loved me as a neighbor (point as if to three distinct persons):
The priest who said, "Can't stop now, sonny"? (hold arms akimbo);
The Levite who said, "Too bad, too bad"? (snap fingers once);
Or the Good Samaritan? (slap hands on thigh).
Go thou (point to one side of the congregation),
And do likewise (swing arm to other side of congregation).

This time we'll retell the story of the Good Samaritan as Jesus might have told it to us today. You now have a feeling for the way the story will be told. So be my echo again and repeat the same words and actions after me.

I am who I am (point to yourself).
One day I put on my shoes (pretend to put on shoes),
And my leather jacket (mimic slipping arms into jacket).
I took my money (open up hand)
And hid it in my jeans pocket (slip hand into back pocket).
Then I got on my ten-speed racer (climb on bike)
And started on my way (race down the road).
From _____ to ____(name two local communities)
Uphill and downhill (lean forward and the backward while still driving the bike),
Past big trees where muggers might hide (look around fearfully),

I pretended I wasn't afraid (big smile).

But all of a sudden (arms go up),

The muggers jumped out at me! (jump off bike, hands shoot up);

One of them hit me (kneel, head down)

That was the last thing I remember (bend further down).

After a while (cup hand to ear and bring head up)

I heard footsteps (cross arms, slap hands on arms).

The footsteps became louder (slap more loudly).

It was a . . . minister (name your own denomination; stop slapping and hold arms akimbo)

He said, "Can't stop now, sonny" (look down and shake head).

"But I'll come back later" (wave good-bye).

After a while (cup hand to ear).

I heard new footsteps (raise hands to shoulder level, snap fingers).

It was a teacher from (name a local school and continue snapping fingers).

She said, "Too bad, too bad" (shake head);

Then she went on her way (wave good-bye).

Soon I heard the sound of a motorcycle (make sound of roaring motor).

It was a tough looking member of the Hell's Angels (step forward and give thumbs up).

Hey! Need any help? (in low growly voice).

Then he jumped down (jump up and down once),

And tore off his leather jacket (pretend to take off coat),

And wrapped it around me (move hands in circular wrapping motion).

Then he lifted me onto his motorcycle (mimic lifting and placing body gently),

And slowly we went on our way (hold hands as if gripping handlebars, make roaring sound of engine).

Until we came to the Holiday Inn (make sound of screeching brakes).

He carried me inside (arms outstretched in carrying position),

Laid me on a bed (pretend to place body on bed),

And paid the manager a hundred dollars (mimic handing out several bills).

"Take care of my buddy," he said (rough, tough voice, one hand outstretched, palm up).

"I'll take care of the cost" (pat back pocket where money would be).

This grizzly looking guy from Hell's Angels went on his way (roar off on the motor bike).

Now I ask you (point finger at audience while the audience points fingers at you)
Which one loved me as a Christian (point to three imaginary people):
The minister who said, "Can't stop now, sonny"? (hold arms akimbo and shake head);
The schoolteacher who said, "Too bad, too bad"? (snap fingers once);
Or the tough looking guy from Hell's Angel's? (grab the handlebars and make the sound of the engine again).
Go thou (point to one side of audience),
And do likewise (sweeping motion to the other side).

8

Essays: First and Last Things

THE SIX ESSAYS IN this chapter combine the religious concerns of the gospel (the Jesus factor, let's say) with an elegant literary style (the Elvis factor, so to speak).

The Greatest Story Ever Told

By Jim Taylor

With apologies to Fulton Oursler's novels (and the movie based on it) for borrowing their title.

In the beginning, there was nothing. Not even darkness. And then, amazingly, out of nothing, a drop of energy formed. As it splashed, space and time were born; dimensions emerged. The energy made light. The energy made heat. Balls of energy melted together, building bigger balls of energy, until those balls could no longer contain all that compressed energy. They exploded and seeded the new universe with the physical elements that still form everything.

Our bodies consist of the atoms created by exploding stars; we are stardust. The echoes of that ancient explosion still ring through the universe; they echo within every cell in every living being. With matter came gravity, the attraction of all things to all things. Free-floating molecules clung together.

The stardust formed gas clouds, galaxies, and stars. One of those stars became our sun. Some of the stardust attracted towards that sun started swirling around it. The dust and debris formed a solar system, with planets. One of those planets, we call our earth.

It began as an utterly inhospitable place, a seething sphere of molten rock. It was not paradise. But as it cooled, some of the gases circulating in its atmosphere blended into something new: water vapor. The vapor condensed into liquid. It fell onto the earth. It ran down over hot rocks and formed streams and rivers, lakes, seas and oceans. In that mineral-rich chemical broth, life emerged. We don't know how it happened, but we know it did, because we're here.

Those first plants, still single cells, absorbed energy streaming from the sun, converted it into chemicals necessary for life. The plant cells grew, and multiplied, and died. When their waste product, free oxygen, threatened to poison life on earth, new life emerged—animals, who used that oxygen to feed themselves.

Each form of life enabled other forms of life. In time, plants and animals both ventured from water onto dry land. Trees and grasses, frogs and lizards, bugs and insects, furry creatures and feathered creatures, grew and multiplied and died, and made room for new plants and animals. In time, we became one of those animals. We call ourselves "humans." This is our story.

We call ourselves intelligent beings, but if there is intelligence, it exists in the collective sentience of all living things. It draws us together, connects us, cautions us, points us into the future. In this great story, we realize we are not created uniquely, distinctly. We are not the goal of creation; we are part of its evolving story.

We are all related. To each other. To all animals. And to all plants, and to the waters where life began, And to the blue planet spinning in the vast network of space, And to the star dust from which we all came. We are children of the universe, and parents to the universe that will succeed us.

We are not alone. We are but a moment, the boundary between what has been and what will be.

Jim Taylor is a lay person who has dedicated most of his life to the church, having served as the managing editor of two magazines, one of them the national publication of the United Church of Canada.

This God Thing

By Catherine Stutt

Faith is weird, and personal, and elusive, and takes a lifetime of pursuit and denial. That's what makes it so special. If there is one single solitary thing in life that absolutely must be unique to a soul, it's faith.

I was baptized in the Anglican Church and still remember the kind face of the priest smiling down from the pulpit of the tiny St. George's Church in Falkenburg, in rural Muskoka. As a teen, I was confirmed in the United Church in Bracebridge, and my heart fills with how readily this farm girl was embraced by the love of the minister and his wife and family.

My husband and I organize the Salvation Army Kettle Campaign in our adopted eastern Ontario town, and we fill the time slots with atheists, agnostics, evangelicals—just good people, many absent of faith or non-faith labels. A good friend is a department head at the local Catholic high school, and each Sunday, he texts photos of his sons enjoying New England Patriot games. Unless of course, the Pats aren't winning, and then there is a prayerful silence for salvation.

Labels are restrictive. Do I need to be a committed church-attending Christian to think the commandments are decent guidelines for a life path? I don't think so. They just make sense in any world.

Do I have to deny the existence of a greater being to be open to secular ideas? Some of my best friends are Christians. Some of my best friends are not. Each of them would answer the phone in the middle of the night and be wherever they were needed.

From early May to late October, I attend and help promote the famed and fabulous Codrington Farmers' Market, our Church of the Agrarians. While attendance swells when church gets out, this is a destination market, a five-mile drive from the nearest house of worship, and—perhaps not so tongue-in-cheek—early visitors have been heard to say they are there for the agnostic shift.

A 96-year-old member of the Order of Eastern Star drives a 95-year-old friend who has been a member of the local Women's Institute and United Church Women for more than 70 years.

In small towns and rural communities across the nation, membership in volunteer organizations is at a critical stage. Masonic Lodges are amalgamating. The Lions and Rotarians are, too. In a nearby county, more than a dozen United Church congregations are desperately trying to find a way to save their buildings. Churches and lodges and halls are becoming more valued as development property than for the faith-based and philanthropic centers they have been, often for a century or more. That's just economics and demographics.

Can we save them? Probably not, but we can preserve their purpose. We can together find a common beacon of goodness. If the Salvation Army and Knights of Columbus and Rotarians and Lions can work together to put coats on kids and food on tables, maybe the idea of faith can return to something less fragmented, less defined by labels, definitions, and denominations.

I honestly don't know if I'm a believer, but I feel I'm a person of faith and hope. When the Patriots are winning, I need neither. When someone I love is in hospital, I need both. Knowing there is an unexplainable presence, an undeniable comfort on the sidelines, a safety net on which I can rely, something neither logic nor science nor proof can explain, the stars shine a little brighter in the troubled night.

Catherine Stutt is a journalist and the editor of County & Quinte Living lifestyle magazine (Prince Edward County, Ontario).

Will God Rescue Us From Climate Disaster?

By Harold Wells

The short answer is no. No one seriously expects that God will suddenly re-freeze the Arctic or blow away the carbon dioxide that we've been dumping into the atmosphere. True, the governor of Texas, in the midst of the worst drought and forest fires in Texas history, publicly prayed for rain, while claiming that climate change is a hoax. But the Creator "who has created and is creating," to quote the United Church creed, does not set aside the rational order of the universe to accommodate human folly. The laws that enable the evolution of life were wondrously fine-tuned into that big bang 14 billion years ago. Coal, oil and natural gas emit carbon dioxide when burned; carbon dioxide in the atmosphere traps heat and will not naturally dissipate for centuries. If the polar regions continue to melt, the planet will warm disastrously. Mass extinction is a real possibility.

It's too late to hide behind "opinions" about this. It's not mere opinion but peer-reviewed science that tells us how greenhouse gases are disrupting the normal patterns of planetary weather. Hundreds of climate scientists of the UN Intergovernmental Panel on Climate Change tell us that the great frequency of weather disturbances—floods, snowstorms, droughts, hurricanes, forest fires, excessive heat (and sometimes excessive cold)—is mainly the result of carbon emissions from human activity in resource extraction, industry, transportation, agriculture, heating and cooling. If we do not act decisively, the crisis will be out of our hands.

We know what to do about it. We must mobilize resources into renewable energy, and power our world in a way that harmonizes with the delicate, interdependent eco-systems of the planet. Making the transition is affordable, practical and immensely beneficial. But will we do it? It's a colossal task and will take a tipping point of public awareness, public demand and political courage. Naomi Klein tells us in her recent book *This Changes Everything* that it will require a transformation of the capitalist system and a dramatic shift toward co-operation—both within and among nations. This is not a scientific matter; it's a moral choice and a profound spiritual challenge. We have begun, but we have a very long way to go.

Is it "sinful" to burn fossil fuels (as we all do)? It's surely not a sin that we clever humans discovered the power of these fuels to deliver levels of prosperity, comfort and health previously unimaginable. However, willful blindness, deliberate lies and denial of facts—to protect profits—are sins indeed.

Fossil fuel dependence can't be turned around on a dime. The great obstacles to the necessary transition to renewables are some of the most powerful people in the world, who profit from fossil fuel industries. Faithfulness to the Creator now means pushing governments for the tax laws, regulations and massive investment that will move us to alternative sources of energy.

God did not quench the forest fires of Texas or dry up the flooding rivers of Alberta. Nor should we expect some supernatural rescue from further climate disasters. Yet we continue to confess: "We believe in God . . . We trust in God."

For Christians, the eternal Source and Ground of all life and power is the Spirit of Gentleness, the self-limiting One whom we have encountered in Jesus Christ. While not overwhelming the autonomy of humanity or the laws of nature, the Creator loves the world and is not absent or indifferent to its struggles. Wonders can be achieved when God "works in us and others by the Spirit." The Spirit acts through prophetic leaders, through movements of committed people, and is marvellously present in the natural processes of healing and restoration. Praying for rain (or for the rain to stop) will not be enough. We will continue to pray and to hope in God as we "live with respect in Creation." Let us also act—personally and politically.

Harold Wells is an ordained minister and theologian of The United Church of Canada. He has taught in Lesotho, Africa and Toronto, Ontario (Emmanuel College).

Held By a God Who Hurts Too

By Bruce McLeod

Our grandson Patrick died on Friday night. He was tobogganing with friends near home a couple of hours north of Toronto, and hit a tree, which broke his heart.

Pat was 17, a bright and smiling boy with untapped abilities edging out like spring leaves, a clear and honest spirit, and a quiet gift for making people of every age around him feel listened to. Like many of the world's best people, he was a young man all his life. His face won't wrinkle, nor his hair fall out. Arthritis won't bend his back, nor will his mouth turn down from years of sliding accommodation to the way things are. For those who love him, he'll always be the promise green of what isn't quite, but might yet be.

The world will never be the same for Joyce and me, the grandparents, and certainly for his parents, Denise and Gary, and for Greg his older brother with whom he is closer than breathing.

Denise phoned to say an ambulance was rushing to Toronto's St. Michael's Emergency. We waited for them there, held them when they came, and felt held by thoughtful nurses, a caring chaplain, and a trauma team doctor who popped her head around a door, said everything was ready, and they would do their best.

As it turned out, Pat didn't make it much past Newmarket Hospital where we finally left him in the middle of the night.

"What then do we say to these things?" asked Paul those years ago. Well, we don't say much. We're not big enough to find the words. Brief visitors, all of us, to this whirling planet, one or another of us always, and all of us sometimes find ourselves, "as on a darkling plain," bewildered by tsunamis, falling aircraft, sudden breast cancer, and toboggans, lethal in the night. And short of explanations.

So in the parking lot we wrapped our arms around each other, and held on, our thoughts flying in all directions like frightened birds.

Do we tell our kids never to go tobogganing, never learn to drive, or fly, never cross the street alone, never grow up? Sometimes we'd like to tell them that, but we can't; they have to grow. But how do they get to 17 so fast?

And would we really prefer a world of puppets and string dolls where toboggans never slam into trees, good people never suffer, and bad people get what they deserve?

God knows the world we have is not like that. Gravity holds us upright; it also takes us down. It's not that easy to stand our ground. And God makes us free to risk, to choose this course or that, to drive fast or slow, to smoke or not, to love or hate, to respect the earth, or trample it to death. It's the world God gives us, and where we grow, or are suddenly gone. What makes it both beautiful and terrifying is that none of us can predict or control what's coming, even as far as suppertime tonight.

But doesn't God send things for a reason? "God took him" we murmur in funeral parlours, imagining it's comforting in the pain to think of God somewhere far off, with a reason in hand. Old-time singer Al Jolson used to mourn his Sonny Boy: "The angels grew lonely; took you, because they were lonely." It sounds religious. However blinding the pain down here, a reason somewhere else, and known only to God.

But it just won't do. Our hearts knew better in the hospital parking lot, arms wrapped round each other, shoring up our common fragility against the storm. "I'm lonely too, Sonny Boy," sobbed Jolson at the song's end. For everyone who finds comfort believing the tragic thing is the will of God, there are a thousand, like Jolson, like Job, who say whatever the reason, it isn't good enough. A God with any reason for inflicting such a pain is an unthinkable God, and not the God we learn about through Jesus in the Bible, not the God we sensed beside us Friday night.

"It is not the will of my father in heaven that one of these little ones should perish," Jesus said. Not the will of God that we should fill our waterways with poison, experiment with genes and bombs and set in motion no one knows what chain effects, that cars should shoot like guns down streets, or a toboggan hurtle headlong down a hill and slam into a tree. It's just the way the world is made, and the way we live and play in it.

As we held each other we sensed beyond our thoughts and prayers and helpless words the presence of another kind of God altogether—the God that Jesus knew. God, like a mother, hands tight behind her back, watching her child cross the street alone for the first time—watching him, almost calling him back to take his hand, yet knowing he mustn't be a child forever, but has to walk freely on his own.

Far from sending the pain, this God, like a mother, is hurt in our hurt. Our tears are on this God's face before we know to weep, this God's love is heartbroken with Patrick at the tree, holding him always, holding also those who waited and didn't know, and vainly hoped. This love is not distant, or unmarked, we learn each Lent before the Cross. Just where we wait and weep, it's clearest seen.

133

There were more arms than ours in the parking lot that night, more than the arms of caring strangers who reached for us with kindness, more than the arms of friends who soon arrived. The love that held us seemed to come through them, not from them.

It came after us in our far country, like a father running down the road to find his son. It came from some deep prior place and held us there on Friday night with love.

Like Jesus came for us from God's own heart to hold us. He told us of the running father. According to the New Testament, he held people all the time. Over and again, it says, he stretched out his arms. He took children in his arms. He held them fast with love.

He still does. With love that didn't begin or end with him. Love that has always been in God's great heart. Love that cloaked creation's chaos from the beginning and has never been erased, though chaos does its worst. Love that is not the explanation or final cause of suffering.

Love that is the permanent presence in God's world that refuses to give suffering the last word—with us in the worst of times, like a mother, hurt in our hurt, weeping with our tears. Holding our rage and our pain and our asking Why. Never letting go, surprising our thin strength over and again with resilience we never guessed ahead of time was there.

"What can separate us from this love?" asked Paul. "Can persecution, distress, famine, danger, or sword? No," he says. "I am sure that neither death nor life, nor things present nor things to come"—not tsunamis, not cancer, not unspeakable losses on any Friday night—"not anything else in all creation will be able to separate us from the love of God, which we know in Christ Jesus."

This is Love that comes from home. "The eternal God is our refuge," says the old verse, "and underneath are the everlasting arms. " They are always there.

"Into your hands I commit my spirit," said Jesus when the dark came in. The hands were there. They held him. They're still there. They held us in the parking lot on Friday night. They hold mothers in Iraq and in Darfur, and in bread lines on our rich streets. They hold the whole wide world. They hold us all, and all we love, in life, in death, in life beyond death. They will never let us go.

Thanks be to God, through Jesus Christ our Lord.

Bruce McLeod is a minister of the United Church of Canada and a former Moderator of the denomination.

134

One Day, I Will Die

By Judith Brocklehurst

One day, I will die.

That doesn't frighten me. I don't know where I'll go, but I know who I'll go to. Dying will be like breaking out of an eggshell.

But there are things about dying that frighten me.

The worst is that people won't be honest with me. I don't want to have to play that horrible game of "you're going to get better" with doctors or my family. There will come a point when "better" means getting rid of the I.V. and the transfusions, and my tired, ugly body, and going on.

I don't want people coming round the door to me with big smiles and small talk, because they've just been told that it's . . . shh . . . well, actually, it's terminal. Where did they get that foul word from: terminal? And that other one: no hope? Don't they know there is a door people go through? Don't they know that our death is full of hope?

I'm frightened of being given treatment without having any honest idea of what the results will be in terms of the quality of life I can expect. I won't need that kind of "help." But I'll need help to leave my family and my friends. I'm afraid of being treated when all I'll need is to be comforted.

I'm frightened that people will concentrate on keeping me "alive" when "alive" means simply breathing. I'm frightened that I won't be given permission to die.

I wouldn't be bothered too much by having to be cleaned up or fed by someone else: the human body isn't a very dignified thing anyway. But the thought of pain bothers me. It would bother me less, if I knew I wouldn't have to depend for pain control on someone else's decisions: if I could be trusted with some say in what medication I got and when I took it. There would be enough to think about, without worrying all the time about when the pain was going to start and what the hell I'd do when it did.

But I'm frightened that, as a dying person, I might become a being to be protected from the truth, from decisions: something less than a human adult. I don't want to be stripped like that.

I'd like to die at home. But if that can't be, I want to die with people around me who are prepared to treat me with the respect I deserve and the tenderness I'll need. Who will talk about what's happening. Realistically. So you're going to die. So what? Death isn't a dirty word.

I'm afraid for my doctor. I'm afraid that he won't want to face me, if we get into a situation where he can't "cure" me. That he'll feel there isn't anything more he can do for me. There will be something more. Help me to die. Tell me I'm still a person. Care about me. Keep me comfortable, if you can. But see me through. Let dying heal me.

They say everyone fantasizes about their own funeral. I don't care what my funeral service is like, but it must be ecumenical.

I've loved and been loved by marvelous Catholics, Anglicans, Presbyterians, United Church people, Eastern Orthodox, atheists, agnostics . . . you name it. I want them all there. Singing "Lord of the Dance" at the tops of their voices.

And afterwards, I want them to have a terrific party. A real bash. Have fun. I did.

Why am I writing about this, when the sun is lighting up the tips of the new lilac shoots and the tiny violets are out in a corner of my garden?

I guess just because it's been such a great ride.

I don't know when my stop will come. I may have to jump off in a hurry before I'm ready, or I may wait around impatiently while everyone else gets off ahead of me.

Part of the strange delight of living is the knowledge that the lilacs will bud, and flower, and seed. It's not going to be this way forever. The human body isn't built for permanence, and life is dynamic, not static.

I'm sure that, whatever "eternal life" is like, it will be more, not less exciting than what we are experiencing now. I'm sure it will be marvelous.

The notion of "everlasting rest" is a horrid one, if it makes you think of something carved in stone on a funeral monument. I prefer to think of the way kids "rest" when they get home tired from school. They shoot out to play . . .

On her deathbed, Lady Hester Stanhope was heard to murmur, repeatedly:

"It has all been very interesting. It has all been very interesting."

You and me, both, Lady Hester. You and me, both.

Judith Brocklehurst was a lay preacher and journalist in Bracebridge, Ontario. She shot out to play in 2008.

What I Believe About the Future Life and Why

By William O. Fennell

I have been asked to give a statement of what I believe about the future life and why. What are the foundations of my Christian hope and what is its content? It is a large subject for such a little space.

As a Christian, my ultimate source of hope, as also of faith and love, is Jesus Christ. It is true, of course, that I have other lesser hopes, as well as other loves than those that derive directly from him. But sooner or later these other hopes and loves founder not only on disappointment but also, and more seriously, on the stark reality of death. For death is a stark reality! Or, better said, death is the end of all reality for the one who dies. Death is the nothing towards which all of us are heading from the moment of our birth. Death indeed is the nothing toward which everything tends.

I share this conviction with today's most sober realists, that death is man's last enemy against whose power he cannot finally prevail. I consider it a noble thing that some of these realists nevertheless commit themselves to battle with all their intelligence and strength against the powers of death—disease, poverty, ignorance and all that robs people of their dignity and worth—even though they know that in the end they and all their efforts must fail. Yet, however noble and worthy of praise their attitude and actions may be, they are not as hopeful and as realistic as God has given them the right to be!

For the end of human possibilities is not the end of possibilities for God. Indeed, the creation of new possibilities for man in the face of death is what the Gospel, the good news of our faith, is all about. In creation God in love called out of nothing a world of beings other than himself and continued in love to give them their power to be. And when through their estrangement from himself they came under the power of the nothing whence they came, God acted once more to restore to them their power to be. Jesus is the one in whom this action most crucially took place. That is why in the Gospels he is called Life and the source of Life and why his work is spoken of as a new creation. God who first gave life gives it again in Jesus through his victory over death and all that makes for death.

The foundation of my Christian hope, then, lies in the faith that the living God has acted in the life that Jesus lived, and the death he died, to recreate for humanity possibilities for life that God willed for us in the beginning but that we lost because we would not seek our power for living from the living God. Jesus' resurrection is the sign and the accomplishment of God's triumph in us over the powers of sin and death.

The content of my Christian hope is that this victory over death will finally triumph over all the things that make for death in us and the world that God has made. All enemies of life at every level of our being—disease of body, the dark, destructive powers of mental illness, the even darker, more destructive powers of formless passion and loveless pride, and their ensuing guilt—will be conquered and destroyed.

But even more than that! We know that here and now, through the grace of God and the skill of men and women, partial victories over these enemies of life are being won. They are partial, for they never are perfect, and they too will end in death. Yet, in some mysterious way, they will be caught up and included in the final victory over evil that is called the kingdom of God. Because of God's triumph over death in Jesus we no longer think it foolish to say "there never will be one lost good." God "will seek again the things that have passed away." In the forgiveness that he has wrought in Jesus, God will judge them and strip them of their evil, and conform and perfect them in their good.

To be sure I am speaking here of mysteries that need a language that can only point at truth without really grasping it. Nevertheless, I find it possible to think these good things about the future because of what God in the past has done for us in Jesus.

Since this, then, is our destiny, and the destiny of all that God has made, we cannot despair though evil in the world is most rampant and death's horror so widespread. Rather we draw from it courage and intention to labor on the side of all who seek death's destruction by fostering life and love and all that serves the human good.

William O. Fennell was a professor of Systematic Theology and Principal of Emmanuel College in Toronto. He died in 2010.

Permissions

In addition to the permissions listed below, special thanks to family and friends for the use of the following poems: "God is Like My Mommy" and "A Shining" by Jim Taylor; "A Valedictory Address to Little People," "Today I Visited Auschwitz," and "Ministers Don't Have Sex on Saturdays" by Sandra McTavish; "The Women" by Anonymous; and "Looking to the Light" by Patricia Wells. Thanks also to E. R. Greenwood, John Weaver, Ron Klusmeier and Walter Farquharson, Bryan Buchan and Barbara Beattie for their musical compositions; to Judith Brocklehurst and Harold Wells for their contribution to the chapter on prayer; to Alastair Dunlop for the picture of "Absent Friends," to Paul Scott Wilson for "A Communion Service," and to Jim Taylor, Catherine Stutt and Judith Brocklehurst for their contributions to the chapter on essays. (James Weldon Johnson's poem "The Creation" was available, we are grateful to say, through the public domain.)

"i am a little church (no great cathedral)". Copyright © 1958, 1986, 1991 by the Trustees for the E. E. Cummings Trust, from COMPLETE POEMS: 1904–1962-by E. E. Cummings, edited by George J. Firmage. Used by permission of Liveright Publishing Corporation;

Weems, Ann. "Where Is the Church?" *Reaching for Rainbows*. The Westminster Press, 1980, pp.77–78;

Weems, Ann. "Christmas Trees and Strawberry Summers." *Reaching for Rainbows*. The Westminster Press, 1980, pp. 29–30;

FRIDAY MORNING
Words: Sydney Carter
© 1960 Stainer & Bell, Ltd. (Admin. Hope Publishing Company, Carol Stream, IL 60188). All rights reserved. Used by permission;

"Who Am I?" From LETTERS AND PAPERS FROM PRISON, REVISED, ENLARGED ED. by Dietrich Bonhoeffer, translated from the German by R.H. Fuller, Frank Clark, et al. Copyright © 1953, 1967, 1971 by SCM Press Ltd. Reprinted with the permission of Scribner, a division of Simon & Schuster, Inc. All rights reserved;

Acknowledgments

I WISH TO ACKNOWLEDGE my indebtedness to Ian McTavish, Sandra McTavish, and Susan Salt Taylor for computer assistance; to Marion McTavish for her patience and insight during this whole process; and not least to Daniel Lanning, George Callihan, Matt Wimer, Joe Delehanty, Shanalea Forrest, and Mike Surber for once again giving Wipf and Stock a good name in the McTavish household.

CPSIA information can be obtained
at www.ICGtesting.com
Printed in the USA
LVHW052357300819
629592LV00007B/45